Giving children the *"expectations"* advantage!

SunBurst Publications

Robert T. Tauber, PhD

[KDP Giving Children 4 23 21]

A valuable resource for parents, teachers, social service providers, and other child-care personnel!

Robert T. Tauber, PhD

Professor Emeritus
The Pennsylvania State University
rtt1@psu.edu

Acknowledgements

I want to acknowledge my wife, Cecelia, for putting up with me when I repeatedly asked, "What do you think about including such and such?" Her responses helped provide focus to this book; her overall editing helped make the book be more readable. By watching her deliver expectation-type messages to me, and to our children, family, friends and neighbors, was a joy to watch, hear and experience. I learned a lot. And, a lot of it is in this book.

I also offer special thanks to our son, David, our daughter, Rebecca, and to our five grandchildren, Sebastian, Olivia, Ethan, Noah and Henry. Individually, as well as collectively, they regularly meet, in fact, exceed my wildest expectations!

A special thanks goes out to Sebastian and Olivia for their creation of several of the cartoon figures that are used to begin selected chapters. Just seeing them makes me smile and I *expect* (the focus of this book) that you will smile, too.

Most of us believe that we achieved or "made it" on our own. We are the ones that read all of those books, attended all those classes, took all of those tests, served all of those internships, etc. But the truth of the matter is that our success hinges greatly on those around us and the expectations-type messages they delivered. Without them, well...., I am not sure I even want to think about it. Let's just say, "Thanks all of you!" (RTT)

Conversational Writing Style

This book is not written as, nor was it intended to be, primarily a piece of scientific literature, complete with an Abstract, Methods, Subjects, Results and Conclusions. You will be spared all those elaborate and seemingly endless charts and graphs that often accompany such scientific articles. Hopefully, you will find this book reader-friendly and immediately useful!

Several humorous and personal stories help teach the concept of the self-fulfilling prophecy. The power of expectations is wielded by us on others AND by others on us. Truly, first impressions are lasting, almost unchangeable, impressions.

Dedication

This book is dedicated to children....what we expect of them....and what, in the end, they will expect of themselves. May both sets of expectations be high. After all, we *expect* the children to be our future.

About the Author

Dr. Robert T. Tauber is certified as a physics teacher, guidance counselor, principal, and school superintendent. His more than thirty-five years' teaching experience includes teaching at an inner-city junior high, counseling at a vocational-technical high school, and teaching courses in educational psychology, foundations of education, human growth & development, management of interpersonal relationships, classroom discipline and democracy at the university level.

Dr. Tauber has supervised teaching interns at both the elementary and secondary levels, and for more than twenty-five years has set up, supervised, and evaluated off-campus field experiences for his teachers-in-training – most often in urban schools.

He has authored many journal articles and published more than 10 books, including, *Classroom Management: Sound Theory and Effective Practice* (4th), from ABC-CLIO publishers. The 3rd edition of this text has been translated into Chinese! His book, *Acting Lessons for Teachers: Using Performance Skills in the Classroom,* is now into its 2nd edition. His book, *Self-Fulfilling Prophecy: A Practical Guide to its Use in Education*, has been repeatedly cited by practitioners and fellow authors.

His most recent book, *Projecting Enthusiasm: The Key to Dynamic Presentations for Professionals*, (2019) has been published by ABC-CLIO. The well referenced, easy to read, and immediately useful book first establishes that "projecting enthusiasm" is the most critical item for presenters, and then goes on to offer specific ways to accomplish it. Among the skills highlighted are animation in body, animation in voice, use of humor, role-playing (by the presenter), use of props, suspense & surprise, space utilization, and creative entrances and exits. Reviewer endorsements are extremely positive!

Dr. Tauber served a six-month sabbatical at the University of Melbourne studying classroom discipline practices in Australia. Prior to that, he served a 10-month sabbatical at Durham University investigating how British educators wield power and influence in the classroom.

Dr. Tauber retired from The Pennsylvania State University with Professor Emeritus status. He and his wife, Cecelia, then relocated to The Villages in Florida where he taught as an Adjunct Professor at the University of Florida in Gainesville, FL. He and his wife have since returned to Pennsylvania, residing at the Masonic Village in Elizabethtown. Feel free to conduct a GOOGLE search of Dr. Tauber's other work. Enter in "Robert T. Tauber."

Preface

Although the title of this book highlights giving *"children"* the expectations advantage, in truth, it is a book about giving *anyone* and *everyone* the expectations advantage. Factors such as age, race, gender, looks, body-build, ethnicity etc., should not matter but, of course, they do. We are all in this world of expectations together. There is no escaping it. The power of expectations, or more specifically, the self-fulfilling prophecy (SFP), is not something that is neutral. It is not something that can, nor should, be ignored. Either it works in your favor OR it works against you. Worse yet, if it starts out working against you, it is likely to stay that way throughout your contact with the expectation's deliverer – teacher, coach, neighbor, boss.

It is not uncommon for teachers to claim that they treat each and every student as a *tabula rasa* or blank slate. These teachers pride themselves in ignoring students' permanent records and other data regarding their soon-to-be classroom of students. In this way, they claim to approach each new class of students with an open mind and without the prejudice inherent in having read the permanent records or quizzed last year's teachers for a "heads up." They are fooling themselves.

If teachers do not "learn" about their students through these time-honored ways, it will take only seconds to form expectations of their students as they walk through the classroom doorway. The teachers will note, among many, many other things, whether the students smile or not, provide eye contact or not, are on time or not, where they choose to sit, how they are dressed, how they are groomed, whether they appear (pencil and notebook) ready to learn, etc.

All these first impressions, at a glance, "tell" teachers what they are likely to expect and, sure as shooting, they will look for evidence to back up their first impressions. And, sure as shooting, they will find that evidence. The eye sees what it wants to see.

There is no way to eliminate the power of expectations. The best that we can do, the purpose of this book, it to help readers understand how the SFP works and recognize the characteristics that trigger expectations in the first place. Once deliverers of expectations understand the SFP process and its triggers, they have a better chance of recognizing it when it occurs and then working to heighten the positive expectations and to dampen the negative expectations.

To write is to sweat! To write is to start off blind about the *expectations* demanded. I suppose that not knowing all of this ahead of time is a blessing. If this were not the case, few would begin the journey at all. For me, this journey has been worth it. I hope that you agree.

Finally, I have kept the research citations to a bare minimum. With today's internet, anyone can look up and secure information on any topic including the power of expectations.

Table of Contents

- Child's Sneakers Untied with Long, Floppy, Laces Dragging on Floor
- Whether a Child Chews Gum
- Whether a Child Chews Snuff
- Whether Child's Parents Provide Snacks when Requested
- Whether Child's Parents Accompany him/her to School the First Day (perhaps, even to the classroom door, itself!)
- Whether Parents Sign and Return Notes, Forms, and Homework Sent Home
- Whether just One or Both of the Child's Parents Come for Parents' Nights
- Whether or Not a Child is Adopted

TWO EXPECTATIONS TRUISMS

"Whether you think (e.g., expect) you can or think you
can't – you are right!"
(Henry Ford)

Henry Ford was right. He captured two powerful truisms. One, "First impressions are lasting impressions!" "Two, you never get a second chance to form a first impression." You have been forewarned; thus, you can be forearmed by reading this book! Your children will thank you!

When teachers are asked, "How many of you think that you are a relatively good judge of character?" because they work so much with people (e.g., kids), most answer "yes." When asked a second question, "How many of you like to be wrong?" Here, they almost overwhelmingly answer that they don't like to be wrong. Think about what has just happened by answering these two questions as they are most often answered.

Respondents who thought they were good judges of character and, at the same time, don't like to be wrong are, in effect, saying that once they have formed a judgment (code word for "expectation"), they have a big stake in that initial judgment or expectation being true. Otherwise, they would have to admit that just maybe they are not as good a judge of character as they first proclaimed. Most of us, including teachers, don't want to make such an admission.

In reality, once teachers have formed an initial judgment, they then actively look for evidence to back up those expectations. They often see as "evidence" what they want to see and, at the same time, ignore evidence that might challenge their initial expectations. Imagine the impact upon a student whose teachers have "pegged" him one way or another, a good student or a slacker, and then set about to find evidence to justify those initial predictions. A child's destiny may already be determined just from the first impressions, and therefore, the lasting impressions, that a teacher has for him or her.

Remember, teachers are human beings first, and teachers, second. Hence, they are not immune to the self-fulfilling prophecy (e.g., the power of expectations) when it comes to their expectations of students. Teachers, like all human beings, will have a tendency to treat some people one way and some people another way depending upon the expectations they hold for those people. Parents should help to insure that teacher expectations of your child are positive.

Although this differential treatment of others appears to be almost a natural thing to do, this treatment can be controlled, in part, by influencing teachers' initial expectations positively and by helping teachers (and others) to understand the self-fulfilling prophecy and how it operates.

WOULD YOU LIKE TO HAVE A PRINCE OR PRINCESS IN YOUR LIFE?

"Treat a man as he is, he will remain so. Treat a man the way he can be and ought to be, and he will become as he can be and should be."
(Goethe)

When I ask this question to various audiences, I usually get a "yes," "yes," "yes," but how? for an answer. I then go on to ask if they know a sure-fired way to achieve this goal. Most people respond by saying that it is impossible to guarantee finding such a person.

Although it may be difficult to "find" such a person, it is quite easy to "grow your own" such person right at home! Yep! You heard me right! You can grow your own prince or princess, but only if you know how to do it.

Now that I have the audience's attention (and perhaps yours, too), I go on to explain what I mean. The fact is that if the power of expectations, in other words, the self-fulfilling prophecy, really works as is claimed in this book, and in the preponderance of expectations research, then the answer to getting a prince or princess in your life is obvious.

Simply treat that special person in your life *as if he or she is a prince or princess* and the odds are very high that the expectations you have of that person will become fulfilled! Does it work every time? Probably not. I do not know of anything that works every single time when it comes to human relationships. But it sure works a lot of the time.

The basis of this book is that we tend to get from other people what we expect of them. By the way, it works in reverse, too. People tend to live up to (or down to) the expectations others hold of them. This is true whether the expectations that we hold are of a child, a student, a worker, or – as in the scenario above – a future prince or a princess.

Try it! What do you have to lose? Better still, read this book and then try it!

WHAT IS SO BAD ABOUT HAVING EXPECTATIONS? SOMETIMES, NOTHING! SOMETIMES, EVERYTHING

"Climate is what we expect, weather is what we get."
Mark Twain

One person has expectations of another. A teacher has expectations for a student. A parent has expectations for a child. A boss has expectations for an employee. This doesn't sound so bad, does it? Not at first glance. In fact, it sounds rather bland and uninteresting. But, let's substitute some possible synonyms for the word "expectations" and then decide whether or not a problem might exist. Woe be the child, student or employee who is on the negative side of any of these words. Why? His or her future is at stake, that's why! He or she could be *your* child.

- **Bias** (as in I had your brother and I know how you probably are going to turn out...)

- **Prejudice** (as in I know about people like you and the likelihood that you will succeed or not...)

- **Outlook** (as in your outlook, based upon such and such, is bright and cheery or it is bleak and dreary...)

- **Disposed** (as in a tendency to do something, I know that people like you cannot help but be...)

- **Anticipation** (as in if I had to bet money, I anticipate that you will be a winner or loser, you will succeed or not succeed...)

- **Probability** (as in I can predict the probability of your success or failure...)

- **Belief** (as in from experience, I believe that you will be a star or be sitting on the bench...)

- **Penchant** (as in a strong and continued inclination, I think you naturally are inclined to do such and such...)

- **Preconception** (as in, you may prove me wrong, but I think that you will turn out this way or that way...)

- **Predisposition** (as in I am predisposed to trust or not trust you...)

- **Proclivity** (as in a tendency to do a particular thing, good or bad is just in your nature…)

- **Prejudge** (as in forming a judgement without adequate information…)

- **Forgone Conclusion** (as in it is a forgone conclusion that you will succeed or fail…)

- **Faith** (I have real faith that you will or will not make it…)

The point of this exercise is to highlight the fact that although the word, *expectations*, itself, does seem all that damming, possible synonyms such as bias, prejudice and foregone conclusions, clearly open the door for misuse by parents, teachers or bosses.

PURPOSE OF THIS BOOK

"When you expect good, it's available constantly, and it makes itself a reality in your life."
(A. Woodward, *Essence*, April 1988)

The purpose of this book is to assist parents (and others) in understanding **and** controlling the power of expectations so they can influence their children's achievement **and** behavior. Most people know a little bit about the Pygmalion Effect, or the idea that one person's expectations can affect the behavior and achievement of another person. This book will teach you much, much more. And, once you learn more about it you can use it to give yourself and those around you the *"expectations"* advantage!

The word "Pygmalion" comes from mythology. Pygmalion was a Greek sculptor who set about sculpting an ivory statue of the perfect woman. While doing so, he fell in love with his own creation and longed for it to become real. Aphrodite, the goddess of love, feeling sorry for

Pygmalion, allowed the statue to came to life. The sculptor's wish – his expectation – was fulfilled.

The volatile up-and-down movement of the stock market is a clear example of the Pygmalion Effect in operation. Investors' expectations control the value of stocks. If investors have high expectations for a particular stock, they will invest in it, thus driving the value of that stock higher. If Warren Buffet is buying such and such stock, so should I! If, on the other hand, these same investors have low expectations of a stock, they will not invest in it, thus driving the value of that stock lower. Hey, if it is not good enough for Buffet, then it is not good enough for me to invest in.

Children, too, are more likely to **soar in value** if their investors – parents and teachers – have high expectations of them. Also, just like the stock market, children can **drop in value** if their investors lose confidence in them. Parents and teachers, as a form of investors, have it within their power to help children achieve and behave appropriately.

Everyone who has seen George Bernard Shaw's play, *Pygmalion,* or viewed the movie *My Fair Lady,* can remember the remarkable transformation in Eliza Doolittle that takes place due to Professor Henry Higgins' beliefs in her (e.g., his expectations). His beliefs in, and his expectations of, Eliza Doolittle helped convince her that she could become a princess. Professor Higgins expected Eliza to become a princess, and with his help – with his positive expectations – she became one. Her transformation became a self-fulfilling prophecy.

Parents can do the same thing with their own children. What is required is a better understanding of how expectations can be positively conveyed in order to benefit children. Unfortunately, few parents understand exactly how to use the Pygmalion Effect, or self-fulfilling prophecy (SFP), as a purposeful tool to convey positive expectations and, at the same time, to avoid conveying negative expectations.

This book aims to provide parents (and others) with this understanding so that they can better control the delivery of expectations in their own homes *and*, perhaps just as importantly, influence teachers' expectations of their children in school.

Consider the implications of the words, **"You never get a second chance to form a first impression!"** Imagine the effect that this truism has on how teachers view your child. Do teachers have your child "sized up," "pegged," or "pigeonholed"? Chances are they do. Once a child has been "pegged," it becomes difficult (but not impossible) to change the teacher's expectations.

As a caring and concerned parent, what can you do to influence these all-important first impressions (e.g., expectations) teachers will have of your child, especially if these expectations are anything other than the "high" or "positive" expectations you want conveyed? This book provides some concrete answers.

People in power, such as teachers in schools and bosses at work, do not like to be seen as being wrong. They like to believe that they can predict, sometimes at just a glance, how a student or employee is likely to turn out in the long run.   Hence, still one more truism, **"First impressions are lasting impressions."**

Some people who hold the destiny of others in the palms of their hands believe that they possess some special innate or acquired ability to predict the future, especially the future of those under them.   These people think that they can predict who will or will not achieve well, and who will or will not behave appropriately.   What these folks in power do not realize is that once they have formed their initial expectations of a student or employee, they actually help these expectations – whether positive or negative – to become fulfilled!

Once those in power have "sized up" or "pegged" a student or employee, they do not want to admit that they may have been wrong.   To admit they have been wrong about "sizing" up someone is to admit that their ability to judge may be flawed.   To admit that they have been wrong about a student or employee is to acknowledge that they may not possess the ability to predict the future as much as they once thought.

Flip Wilson, the late comedian who played the role of Geraldine, regularly proclaimed, "What you see is what you get!" With respect to the subject of this book, it could be said, "What you expect, you usually get." Expect little in the way of positive achievement and behavior from a child and that is, sadly, exactly what you likely will get. But, expect a lot in the way of achievement and behavior from a child and that is what you often will get.

Through the expectations they hold, and then act upon, parents and teachers serve as an important Pygmalion for their children.   But the real goal of understanding and using the power of positive expectations is to influence children's achievement and behavior so that they can become their own Pygmalion. It is similar to the popular children's story, *The Little Engine that Could.*

In the book, the little engine starts off a little low in self-confidence, saying, "I think I can, I think I can, I think I can." Soon, through the positive expectations conveyed by those around it, the little engine builds its self-confidence and soon chugs proudly, "I know I can!" The little engine has become its own life-long Pygmalion. This is what parents want for their own children. This is what teachers want for their students. This is what bosses want for their employees.

This book focuses upon helping parents learn how to convey positive expectations regarding their children's achievement and behavior. Although the focus of this book is upon what parents can do to heighten *expectations* in the home, it later addresses what parents can do to influence the *expectations* of their children's teachers!

I would like to offer still one more truism. In real estate, the three most important words are *"location, location, location."* In parenting and in teaching, the three most important words may well be *"expectations, expectations, expectations,"* hence, the still greater importance of what is contained in this book!

As Francis Bacon said in 1597, "Knowledge is Power!" This statement is as true today as it was centuries ago. This book can make you a more knowledgeable and, thus, a more powerful influence in your child's life.

Now here is something to get you thinking. What do a duck and an elephant have in common? At first glance, perhaps very little. Then, again, upon closer inspection they may have a lot in common. Have you ever heard the saying, "If it walks like a duck and quacks like a duck, then it probably is a duck," or the other saying, "If it feels like an elephant and smells like an elephant, then it probably is an elephant."

What does this have to do with teachers' perceptions of children? Lots! If a child "looks" like a potential scholar, "acts" like a potential scholar, and "sounds" like a scholar, then he or she probably will turn out to be a scholar – at least in the mind of a teacher As a parent, you have it in your power to help your child, "walk the walk" and "talk the talk" of a scholar such that early on teachers will form initial and lasting, positive, expectations of him or her.

"YOUR DAUGHTER HAS FALLEN IN WITH THE WRONG CROWD!"

"The expectation of an unpleasantness is more terrible than the thing itself."
(M. Bashkirteff, *The Journal of a Young Artist*, 1919)

"Your daughter Becky has fallen in with the wrong crowd!" These were the words that our daughter's teacher whispered to my wife and me when we met with her for the first teacher-parent conference of the school year. Actually, we were attending a conference for our son David when his teacher said, "Oh. You are the parents of Becky Tauber, aren't you?" Apparently, this teacher traveled between schools and taught both our son and daughter.

My wife and I did not know what to think. We were alarmed. Here we were on sabbatical in Melbourne, Australia, far, far away from home hearing, and certainly imagining, the worst. Was our daughter into drugs? Was she in a gang? Was she part of an extortion ring? What did her teacher mean by "falling in with the wrong crowd"?

The teacher went on to explain herself. What she meant by "wrong crowd" was that Becky, 14 years old at the time, had been befriended by a group of "non-studiers," and by virtue of being seen with them was assumed (Assume = makes an "ass" out of "u" and "me") also to be a non-studier. I suppose the teacher believed the old adage, "birds of a feather stick together." Note, when you are the new kid on the block, 10,500 miles from home, you don't have a lot of say or control over who does or does not befriend you.

For the initial grading period of the semester in Australia, Becky brought home her first ever "B," her grade in Australian history. The teacher assumed that if Becky was hanging around with these known "non-studiers" then she, too, must be a non-studier.

Nothing could be further from the truth. Becky had had, to that point in her academic career, an outstanding record during her elementary and secondary schooling here in the United States. It took until her last grading period while attending school in Australia for her work to be recognized by this same teacher as "A." Becky went on to attend a major state university on an academic scholarship. Presently, she is a board-certified Radiologist. Have you or someone you know had a similar experience?

Later discussions with this teacher revealed that she somehow knew that I was serving an academic sabbatical at Melbourne University and, as such, must have a healthy respect for the value of education – a belief that surely would have been conveyed to our children. The teacher thought it was her "duty," as a fellow educator, to clue my wife and me in on the situation because she was sure that we would want to catch any such problems in the bud. I suspect that this same teacher did not take the extra time to clue in less-educated parents about similar (e.g., hanging around with non-studiers) problems with their children.

Although specific suggestions will be offered later regarding what you can do to influence the expectations those in power hold over your child, a truism that relates to the story above is that "we are judged (e.g., expectations are formed of us) by the company we keep." It may not be fair, but it is a cold, cruel, fact of life. Help your child to choose his or her friends very carefully!

Who your children hang around with not only impacts the expectations others have for them, but also can influence their daily thoughts, goals and aspirations. If your children hang out with friends who have a mindset that education is important, that a balance must be struck between competing forces (e.g., studies, sports, relationships) and that post-secondary education is important, their daily thoughts and interactions will reflect this attitude.

Daily conversations with similarly motivated people will be future oriented, will focus on planning, will explore options – making them move closer to being the CEO (Chief Executive Officer) of their life. Others around them will take notice and this will contribute to still higher expectations being formed of, and conveyed to, them. It is a bit like a snowball rolling down a hill. Once it starts, admittedly small in the beginning, it gains momentum and size as it rolls along.

YOUR TURN NOW

"A master can tell you what he expects of you. A teacher,
though, awakens you own expectations."
(Patricia Neal)

Now that I have relayed a personal expectations
story regarding my family, our daughter's experience in an
Australian school, how about you doing some soul-
searching of your own. Take a hard look at your own
family.

How do you think teachers view your child(ren).
Try to be as honest as possible in answering the following
questions. Honest answers can give you a clearer view of
reality and provide direction for constructive changes – if
required!

- What do teachers THINK (e.g., what expectations do
  they form) when they see your child? Is this what you
  want them to think?

- What do teachers THINK (e.g., what expectations do they form) when they hear your child speak? Is this what you want them to think?

- What do teachers THINK (e.g., what expectations do they form) when they smell your child? Sorry folks, but kids, just like adults, are human. They can smell good (e.g., fresh and clean) or they can smell bad. Is this what you want them to think?

- What do teachers THINK (e.g., what expectations do they form) when they see, hear, and, yes, smell you? Is this what you want them to think?

- What do teachers THINK (e.g., what expectations do they form) when they note that you did not show up for the scheduled parents' night? Is this what you want them to think?

I hope that you do not see these questions as being insensitive. I agree that how you or your child looks, speaks, or smells should not have a bearing on your child's success in school, but it just ain't (ain't, for emphasis) that way. I also hope that you do not feel like shooting the messenger – me, for sharing with you what I have come to know and learn about the all-important topic of expectations!

DON'T JUDGE A BOOK
BY ITS COVER

"I hope that you don't let anyone else's expectations direct
the course of your life."
(Julianne Donaldson)

But, the world – including teachers – too often does! The "cover," the part people first see, conveys volumes and it does so in a moment's notice – just about the amount of time it takes for teachers to form expectations! Parents should help their child project the best "cover" possible.

If I had a nickel for every time I have heard someone make this statement – "Don't judge a book by its cover," I would be millionaire! But if I had a nickel for every time I have observed someone actually "judging a book by its cover" I would be a billionaire!

I see it in the browsing section of a library. Patrons look at the cover or DVD jacket and decide right then and there whether the book or DVD is worth signing out. I see it at newsstands where customers glance at just the cover and decide whether the magazine is worth buying. I see it in supermarkets where customers scan shelves that are full of different products and decide, after just a brief examination of the front of the boxes (e.g., equivalent to a book's cover), to purchase one product and ignore all of the others. We regularly "judge books (and all other products) by their covers!"

Children (and adults) are like books, their worth constantly is being judged, at least at first, by their "covers." Yet, looks can be deceiving. Their "covers" take many forms, their name, their dialect, their gender, their race, their body build, their degree of attractiveness! An attractive book jacket on a book, a flashy cover on a magazine, or an eye-catching front to a box of detergent or cereal, all contribute to judgments regarding the worth of what is inside. It is not fair, but it happens, and it happens with great regularity! It's even less fair when it happens to children.

As your author, I reviewed information provided by Amazon on how to publish something though Kindle Direct Publishing (KDP), and I was struck by the emphasis that was placed on selecting or constructing an eye-catching cover. I knew it was important, but I didn't believe that it was *THAT* important. In my case, if you hadn't picked up this book and examined it, it is unlikely that I would ever had had a chance to engage, inform and challenge you regarding the power of expectations. The cover of a book or a box of cereal helps get a "buyer's" foot in the door. Maybe, just maybe, they will buy the product.

AN ACORN DOES NOT FALL FAR FROM THE TREE

"You see what you expect to see, Severus."
(J. K. Rowling)

Another well-known saying that relates to the power of expectations is, "an acorn does not fall far from the tree." What this means, at least to some teachers, is that children (e.g., the acorns) are not expected to be all that much different than their parents (e.g., the tree) and/or from their siblings. "Like father, like son," is another way of saying much the same thing. If teachers know something about a child's parents or siblings, then they have every reason to believe (at least in their mind) that they know something about the child himself or herself! This could work to a child's benefit or it could work to his or her detriment! It all depends upon the expectations that the teacher has formed of the child's parents and/or siblings!

Our daughter, Rebecca, followed our son, David by one year in school. David smoothed the road ahead for

Rebecca. He was a good student, good looking, athletic and personable – all characteristics that teachers like in a student. He was respectful, fun to be around and enjoyed both school and the academic challenges it offered. "Oh, (in a positive tone), you are David's sister," was uttered by her teachers. It was clear, although just meeting Rebecca, that her teachers felt that they already knew scads of information about her. After all, she was David's sister and the daughter of Dr. and Mrs. Tauber.

Who among you have been the equivalent of "David" and paved a relatively smooth road for siblings who followed? Who among you clearly were not the equivalent of "David" and, thus, pave a rather rocky road for siblings who followed? What is your story about being a siblings who traveled either the smooth or rocky road prepared for by your older brother or sister?

The acorn falling from the tree mirrors the saying, "Birds of a feather flock together." Nowhere is this more true that where my wife and I live in The Villages, an active over 55 community in central Florida. All 125,000 of the residents basically look the same, most often white with graying hair and a bit of a pudge around the middle, swim in identical 100 heated swimming pools, live in similar (some smaller, some larger) one-story homes, play golf, pickleball or tennis, and are members of still smaller sets of "flocks" – belonging to one or more of the over 3000 clubs.

TRY OUT YOUR EXPECTATIONS: AN EXERCISE

"Anticipate the good so you may enjoy it."
(Congo)

How many of you believe that you are reasonably good judges of character? With years of experience under your belt, are you more often than not able to size up other people correctly? Sure, occasionally you are wrong, but most often you are correct. Right? Whether meeting someone new at a party or greeting a new neighbor or that neighbor's child, can't you sometimes, just at a glance, predict pretty well how certain people are likely, over time, to turn out?

Try the following exercise.

Pretend that you are not reading a book designed to make you more sensitive to the power of expectations. Instead, jot down the first descriptive thoughts that come to your mind when you think about the following kinds of people. Be honest, now. Only you will see what you write. Space has been provided immediately below each item.

Generally, what descriptors might you use to characterize:

- a teenager from a family that has strong and vocal Democratic Party ties.

- a teenager from a family that has strong and vocal Republican Party ties.

- a significantly overweight teenage girl who lives down the street.

- a nine-year old boy of affluent parents two streets over who you know is an *only* child.

- an Asian child down the street who is the son of a respected university math professor.

- an uncoordinated teenage boy in the neighborhood who is thin, almost frail, and very, very short for his age.

- a neighborhood teenage girl whose life seems to revolve around boys, boys, boys.

- an elementary school child who, as you overhear at the supermarket checkout counter, has at least six known siblings and who lives with his divorced and currently pregnant mother who is on welfare.

In spite of your best efforts to resist making predictions regarding these children and their academic or behavioral future, did you catch yourself forming expectations – even fleetingly? Did you catch yourself making predictions about how some of these kids likely will act or will turn out? If your answer is "yes," then you have set the self-fulfilling prophecy in motion. It happens this easily, this quickly! And, it probably is happening in classrooms throughout the country. It probably is happening to your child in his or her school!

This brief "survey" has been duplicated over and over, and published over and over. Personally, although I designed the questions, I never thought that they were all that worthy of such duplication.

TEACHERS' EXPECTATIONS OF HIGH SCHOOL CHEERLEADERS AND JOCKS

"Aerodynamically the bumblebee shouldn't be able to fly,
but the bumblebee
doesn't know that so it goes on flying anyway."
(Mary Kay Ash)

When a group of pre-service teachers were asked to write the first thing that came to their mind when thinking of a "high school cheerleader," the following expectations emerged: "brain-dead, Barbie doll," "someone who is stupid, dumb," "popular and bouncy," "brainless, social butterfly," "air head, studies with jocks for history," "attractive, but unintelligent," "flighty, dumb blond, laughs a lot," 'ditz, blond, definitely not an Einstein," and "thinks she is better than everyone else."

The same respondents expected a "jock" to be "disinterested, if he understands at all," "someone else doing his homework," "slacker, not too bright," "slow person, probably sleeping through class," "has test file from fraternity, just getting a passing grade," "underachiever, loves to party," and "probably not doing too well."

You and I both realize that these expectations are not always true, perhaps, hardly ever actually true. But in the minds of some teachers, they are true often enough that generalized expectations can be formed. If teachers go on to treat students according to these expectations, some real damage can be done.

What Can You Do?

Learn more about the power of expectations. Read the rest of this book. Use this knowledge to give your child the *"expectations"* advantage – at home and at school.

HISTORY OF THE SELF-FULFILLING PROPHECY

"Unhappiness is best defined as the difference between our talents and our expectations."
(Edward de Bono, *The Observer*, June, 1977)

It is usually acknowledged that the term "self-fulfilling prophecy" or SFP, was first coined by sociologist Robert K. Merton in a 1948 *Antioch Review* article titled "The Self-Fulfilling Prophecy." As part of his explanation of the SFP, Merton drew upon a fellow sociologist's theorem: "If men define situations as real, they are real in their consequences" (Thomas, *The Child in America*, 1928, p. 257).

Years later, Robert Rosenthal, a professor from Harvard University, revived the public's interest in the self-fulfilling prophecy when he described a study done with his graduate students. In this study, psychology students were given one of two types of rats, designated "maze-dull" or "maze-bright," to run through a series of maze experiments.

Students with the maze-bright rats were told that their rats would perform normally at first, but, thereafter, their performance would improve markedly. The students with the maze-dull rats were told that their rats were not expected to show much evidence of learning. In reality, the rats had been assigned to student experimenters on a random basis – any differences among the rats existed only in the student experimenters' minds (e.g., their expectations).

By the end of the five-day study, the maze-bright rats had, in fact, performed significantly better than the maze-dull rats. Perhaps more important than how well the rats actually performed was how the student experimenters rated (described) the rats. Maze-bright rat handlers rated their rats more favorably (e.g., described them as being brighter, tamer, and more pleasant). Apparently, even rats can pick up on, and respond to, the expectations (negative or positive) of their caregivers. Would children in a classroom respond the same way?

Rosenthal's follow-up experiment, this time with children, which was reported in the book, *Pygmalion in the Classroom,* did much to call attention to the SFP among educators. In this book, he and his co-author Lenore Jacobson (elementary school principal) describe an experiment where elementary teachers' expectations of students were manipulated. The two researchers led the teachers in eighteen classrooms to believe that approximately twenty-percent of their students were expected to "bloom" academically and intellectually during the school year.

Of course, there never actually was any scientific basis for identifying which students were designated to bloom. Instead, the designated student "bloomers" were randomly assigned so that the only differences between the bloomers and the rest of the student body were in the minds of the teachers. At the end of the year, the students designated as "bloomers" did, in fact, show intellectual gains!

Upon completion of the school year, when asked to describe the classroom behavior of their students, the "bloomers," from whom intellectual growth was expected were described positively by their teachers – having a greater chance of being successful in life, as being happier, more curious, more interesting, more appealing, and better adjusted. On the other hand, when the students designated as non-bloomers bloomed, and some did, these same teachers described these students negatively – less likable, less likely to succeed in life, less happy. It was almost as if the teachers were thinking, "How dare a student achieve if I did not expect him or her to!"

It is a scary thought to know that your child's future may be determined by the expectations that a teacher holds of him or her. Maybe parents need to keep their fingers crossed that their children are not among the students seen by teachers as the equivalent of "non-bloomers," the child equivalent of "maze-dull" rats. Better still, parents could learn more about how to control expectations as they impact their children's lives.

WHAT IS HIDING JUST AROUND THE CORNER

"In this world there is always danger for those who are afraid of it."
(Ralph Waldo Emerson)

Why do human beings seem to have such an investment in the power of expectations, or scientifically better known, the Pygmalion Effect? It all boils down to the need for safety and survival. Recall Abraham Maslow's famous pyramid of needs from Physiological Needs at the bottom (air, food, water), to Safety & Security, to Belonging, to Esteem and, finally, at the top, Self-Actualization. Implied in the hierarchy is that lower needs must either be satisfied, or be seen as well on their way to being met, before attention will be directed to higher needs. Hence, the need for Safety and Security must be addressed early on AND, because none of the lower needs are ever met once and for all, they must be met and re-met over and over. Thus, both initial attention and continued attention must be directed towards establishing and keeping shored up the Safety and Security needs.

How does this apply to our topic of expectations? Human beings are, compared to much of the rest of the animal kingdom, rather ill-prepared to face what could be a dangerous future. What we lack in strength, eyesight, hearing and cunning, we make up for in planning. We tend to plan for the future and sometimes that future is just down the block where a dark alley intersects our sidewalk. We know from experience (our own or from others) that someone could be lurking in the alley ready to pounce and mug us. Probably not, but the thought is still there. We have all seen endless *Law and Order* television programs.

We progress down the sidewalk with the expectation that something might happen. It probably will not happen, but it might. We stiffen, try to look larger, hold our car keys with the pointy ends sticking out. Or, we may well decide to cross the street where it is better lit. Our ability to predict and deal with the expected and the unexpected has allowed mankind to survive and thrive since the beginning of time.

On a less menacing level, take a woman at a bar who is approached by a man who seems keen on chatting her up. As he approaches, her expectation's radar turns on. She sizes him up. Is that a wedding ring on his finger? Is that an outline of where there was, until minutes ago, a wedding ring? Is that a Hell's Angel t-shirt he is wearing? Does he look like he has already had a few too many drinks? All of this is taking place in just moments. Luckily, the young lady has had lots of practice dealing with her expectations and, hopefully, will make the right call.

Given the overload of information, demands and bodies facing teachers at the start of a school year it is no wonder that they try to simplify and compartmentalize incoming data. If a teacher knows, for instance, that her early afternoon math class, right after lunch, is for those who are repeating the class, then it might seem natural to *expect* that all of the students will be in need of remedial help. She also might *expect* the students to be less than enthusiastic about the subject matter. Hence, 30 students worth of information is compartmentalized into just one *expectation* – it will be a demanding class.

On the contrary, if the teacher sees that she is scheduled to teach an advanced-placement literature class, a subject near and dear to her heart, she would start to form high-*expectations* thoughts. She *expects* that the class will be the highlight of her day. She *expects* that she will have students who really want to learn. She *expects* that she will have to spend extra time and energy preparing lessons for these sharp students. Just guess where she will get that extra time and energy. It has to come from somewhere.

The bottom line is that human beings use expectations to survive and to thrive!

PERSONALIZING THE SELF-FULFILLING PROPHECY

"Whatever we expect with confidence becomes our own
self-fulfilling prophecy."
(Brian Tracy)

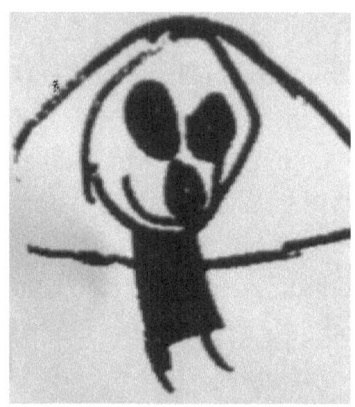

Provide an example of how the self-fulfilling prophecy
(e.g., the power of expectations) was used on you or, if
you have children, was used on one of them.

- What specific expectation has another person held
  of you (or of your child)?   The other person
  expected you (or your child) to......

- Who was the person who held this expectation of
  you (or of your child)?

- What specific characteristic(s) about you (or about your child) do you believe "triggered" these expectations in the mind of the other person?

- Specifically, how were you (or your child) treated differently based upon the expectations held of you (or your child)?

- Did these expectations work to your (or to your child's) benefit or detriment? Explain!

- If the other person held negative expectations of you (or of your child) were you ever able to change those expectations to positive expectations?

- If "yes," how did you do it? If "no," why not?

EXPECTATIONS START AT HOME

"Children respond to the expectations of their
environment."
(W. Grier & P. Cobb, *Black Rage,* 1968)

Expectations start at home. Children at a very young age learn what is and what is not expected of them. Parents play a primary role in conveying these expectations. After all, infants and very young children have no real sense of self, no sense of who they are, and certainly no sense of what they are capable of becoming. They are in the process of forming who they are. Erik Erikson, a famous psychologist, calls this process the forming of an "identity."

Will this identity include being a scholar, being a creative problem solver, being a devoted family member, being successful at a career? The answer to these questions depends a lot upon the millions of expectations messages sent to children during their formative years.

These crucial messages are conveyed to children first by their parents and, later, by others such as grandparents, siblings, peers, neighbors and friends. Later, teachers become another important conveyor of expectations. And, still later in life, employers add their "two cents" worth, or more, of expectations.

- *Expect* (and convey this expectation) your child to do his or her homework and, more than likely, it will get done.

- *Expect* (and convey this expectation) your child to complete his or her daily or weekend chores, and more than likely, they will be done.

- *Expect* (and convey this expectation) your child to go to bed on time and, more than likely, he or she will.

- *Expect* (and convey this expectation) your child to share his or her toys with a sibling and, more than likely, he or she will.

- *Expect* (and convey this expectation) your teenager to be home at an agreed-upon time and, more than likely, he or she will.

- *Expect* (and convey this expectation) your teenager to drive responsibly and, more than likely, he or she will.

- *Expect* (and convey this expectation) your child to develop a sense of independence (or dependence, for that matter) and, more than likely, he or she will.

- *Expect* (and convey this expectation) your child to be responsible, whether with school work, feeding the family pet, keeping his or her room clean, etc.

Now, is expecting something enough? Not really. If this were true, then I would have a yellow Jaguar, V-12, sitting out in my driveway. I don't have one even though I have been expecting one ever since I asked my children to request it on my behalf from Santa Claus each time they sat on his lap at Christmas. Our children are now about 40 years old! But if positive expectations are accompanied by parental behaviors (words and body language) that convey these expectations, then the odds are very high that the expectations will be realized – will be fulfilled!

As powerful a tool as expectations are, no parenting tool is absolutely perfect. As parents, we are playing the odds. The parenting information and skills presented in this book work **most** of the time, with **most** children, in **most** situations.

"What can you do to change teachers' expectations of your child if you have reason to believe that these expectations are anything other than the "high" or "positive" expectations you want conveyed?" One answer is to start at home. Deliver positive expectations! Deliver lots of them!

HOW THE SELF-FULFILLING PROPHECY WORKS

"No one rises to low expectations."
(Les Brown, Motivational Speaker)

·

"I think I can. I think I can. Because you think I can, I know I can!"

First and foremost, the self-fulfilling prophecy (SFP) is a process – a four-step process. **Each step can be controlled by parents, but parents must be informed.** Informed or not, the SFP will continue to operate. Surely it is better to have the SFP operate under parents' direct control.

The four steps in the self-fulfilling prophecy process are listed below and then discussed in more detail. Although the word "teacher" has been used in each of the four steps, one could just as easily substitute other words such as "parent" or "boss." The steps are deceptively simple, especially for the amount of good or bad that can result from the application of this SFP process. You should not only learn these four steps; you should examine your own home environment for instances where the steps in the self-fulfilling prophecy are occurring!

Four-step Self-Fulfilling Prophecy Process

- **STEP 1** - Teacher forms expectations

- **STEP 2** - Based upon these expectations, the teacher treats each child differently

- **STEP 3** - The teacher's treatment tells the child what *behavior* and *achievement* the teacher expects

- **STEP 4** - With time, the child's behavior and achievement will conform more and more closely to that expected of him or her

STEP 1 - Forming Expectations

Most people do not like to face the future with any more unknowns in their life than they have to. Therefore, we form expectations as a way of predicting what is normally an unpredictable future. The most surprising point about the first step in the self-fulfilling process *is not* that people form expectations, but that they form these expectations on factors that ought to have little or nothing to do with a child's future achievement and behavior.

There is a significant body of SFP research that shows that people form expectations of others on such human characteristics as body build, gender, race, ethnicity, given name and/or surname, attractiveness, dialect and/or primary language, and socioeconomic level. Many of these characteristics that can trigger expectations in the minds of others will be discussed.

As you read further, be prepared for some real surprises. You may not like what you read because it will not, in many instances, seem "fair." Fair or not, these various and sundry human characteristics do trigger expectations, including expectations of your child!

Knowing that certain characteristics about your child can influence the expectations others hold of him or her can go a long way in helping you, as a loving and caring parent, to better control these expectations so that they will benefit, rather than possibly harm, your child.

STEP 2 - Treating Children Differently

Different expectations usually lead to different treatments. How does one person convey his or her expectations to another person? How do teachers convey their expectations to students? Expectations are conveyed using four factors including *Climate*, *Feedback*, *Input*, and *Output*.

- *Climate* refers to the emotional mood or spirit, often communicated nonverbally (e.g., smiling or nodding more often, providing greater eye contact, leaning closer to the student) by the person holding the expectation. A more positive climate is produced by teachers for high expectations students – and it is picked up or sensed by these students.

- *Feedback* refers to providing affective information, e.g., more praise and less criticism of high-expectation students, and more cognitive information, e.g., more detailed, as well as higher quality feedback as to the correctness of high-expectation students' responses. Examples would be providing more oral comments to high expectations students' answers in class or more detailed written comments on students' submitted papers.

- *Input* translates into the fact that teachers tend to teach more to students of whom they expect more. For instance, teachers are likely to call aside a high expectations student and offer additional resources that may be helpful in completing assignments.

- *Output* is where teachers encourage greater responsiveness from those students of whom they expect more. Teachers can use their verbal and/or nonverbal behaviors to signal how much response – lots or little – they expect from which students. Examples include providing high expectations students with greater opportunities to seek clarification and asking these students more often for "their opinion" in a class discussion.

STEP 3 - Expectations regarding expected behavior and achievement

Behavior and achievement are the two most important ongoing factors that are judged in the life of a person – whether at home, in school, or in the workplace. Mess either one of them up and disaster can loom on the horizon. Parents judge these two factors over a lifetime. Teachers judge these factors throughout a child's schooling. Employers judge these factors throughout an employee's (professional or blue-collar) career.

Verbal and nonverbal behaviors of a teacher clearly convey to students what future behavior (good or bad) and what future achievement (high or low) the teacher expects of the students. Children, like most young in the animal kingdom, are uncanny in their perceptiveness or their ability to sense what others expect from them. Once expectations are "sensed," they may well be met!

Think back upon your own life. Couldn't you "tell" what your parents expected from you? Couldn't you "tell" what your teachers expected from you? If you are employed, can't you "tell" what your employer expects from you? The message of what others expect from you comes through even more loud and clear because not only do you see how you are treated, but you also have an opportunity to see how those around you are being treated. It didn't take long for you, and I guarantee it doesn't take long for children, to sense what behaviors and levels of achievement are expected from them.

STEP 4 - With time, the child's behavior and achievement will conform more and more closely to that expected of him or her

If day in and day out, year in and year out, children hear the same positive (or negative) expectations conveyed to them, they will soon begin to internalize the message. Because the expectations message they repeatedly hear may well be the **only** expectations messages they hear, they have little choice but to begin to believe that message.

Imagine coming from a home where for all of one's life one has had nothing but negative expectations conveyed. Imagine being in school where for twelve years (plus kindergarten) one has had nothing but negative expectations conveyed. It would be little wonder, then, that one's behavior (good or bad) and level of achievement (high or low) would conform more and more to what was expected from him or her! Hence, a sad, but true ending to this story!

On a brighter note, imagine coming from a home and a school where for all of one's life one has had nothing but sincere and positive expectations conveyed. Here, too, one's behavior and achievement would conform more and more to what was expected from him or her. Hence, there is a happy ending to the story.

Parents and teachers have control over each of the four steps – especially the first two steps – in the self-fulfilling prophecy process. They can (and should) become more aware of the human characteristics that trigger expectations and be on guard for them. They can better control their tendencies to treat children differently based upon the expectations they may hold. In other words, they can control the *Climate*, *Feedback*, *Input*, and *Output* that they provide to children. Are you aware of the *Climate*, *Feedback*, *Input*, and *Output* that you, as well as your child's teachers, are communicating? Shouldn't you be?

HUMAN CHARACTERISTICS CAN TRIGGER EXPECTATIONS

"Dear Mary. We all knew you had it in you."
(Dorothy Parker, Telegram to a pregnant friend)

Each of the following sections identifies a specific human characteristic (e.g., body build, given name, ethnicity) and then describes the expectations this characteristic is likely to trigger in the minds of others – including teachers. While reading about each of these human characteristics, think of your child and imagine the expectations that others may form of him or her based upon these characteristics.

Further, begin to think what you could do as a parent to help mitigate (e.g., control or offset) any negative impact of these expectation-triggering factors if they apply to your child. Think further about how you could enhance any positive impact of these factors. Jot down your ideas while they are hot! It hardly needs to be said, but I will say it – work on changing those things about your child (and yourself) that do not compromise your fundamental beliefs.

Keep in mind the famous Serenity prayer. "God grant me the serenity to accept those things that I cannot change, the courage to change those things that I can, and the wisdom to know the difference." Perhaps it will help as you move forward.

Surely you will catch yourself shaking your head in amazement that so many of us (you and I, included) use these human characteristics as a basis for forming expectations of others. Although I am not happy with the fact that I am as tempted as the next person to "size up" people, I take some consolation in the fact that because I understand how the self-fulfilling prophecy works, I can better control any tendencies to misuse the SFP. Better still, because I understand how the SFP works, I can begin to make the process work for me and for my loved ones!

Although volumes could be dedicated to each expectation-triggering factor, space limitations demand that we limit the discussion to several pages for each factor. This should be enough to convince you to be on the alert to both the damage and the good that can come from exploiting each expectation-triggering factor.

You, too, can make the self-fulfilling process work for you and for the most precious people in your life – your children. Please read further and, while doing so, keep in mind how the material **might** apply to your child(ren)!

GIVEN NAME

"No, Groucho is not my real name. I'm breaking it in for a friend."
(Groucho Marx, Comedian)

All of the following are "real" names. What pictures come to mind when you hear them? But, more importantly, what pictures do you think come to the mind of teachers – often white, middle-class females – when they hear or see these names? After all, first impressions are lasting impressions, aren't they?

Apple, Blanket, Zeke, Winthrop, Gorgeous, Sylvan, Jules, Emily, Erwin, Derek, Tuira, Tobit, Olive, Norma, Mara, Melanie, Linda, Lois, Jackie, Joyce, Honey, Holiday, Edie, Duba, Bambi, Yoel, Victor, Tyron, Todd, Nyasia, Jazmyne, Aubrie, Brionna, Astrid, Abril, Ean, Osbaldo, Braulio, Teddy, Ronald, Rolfe, Heavan, Quentin, Horatio, Gary, Dick, David, Austin, Avner, Nathan, Neil, Ned, Louis, Loretta, Lola, Kelvontain,

Israel, Hannah, Humphrey, Guenevere, Grizel, Eunice, Denzil, Dermot, Desmond, Calista (peaked in 1999 with the television program, *Ally McBeal Show*), Clare, Quazek, Clarence, Haylee, Keanu, Xzavier, Destini, Barnard, Essence, Lexus, Precious, Heaven, Unique, Basil, Jerry, Jacob, Hack, Tiffany, Tilly, Sybil, Sandy, Raoul, Percy, Sir, Peg, Penelope, Madison (our son's middle name), Madisyn, Madyson, Gentle, Micah, Methuselah, Mildred, Miles, Jewel, Diamond, Ruby, Marcus, Lancelot, Quantavious, Lawrence, Larry, Nyah, Destinee, Crystal Ball, Shyanne, Julian, June, Justin, Janet, Jarvis, Judy, Ira, Iris, Hilda, Hippolytus, Peter Pan, Hildegard, Georgiana, Peace, Eveleen, Evan, Sigmund, Natividad, Tariq, Ahmad, Litzy, Tyshawn, Kaitlyn, Jazlyn, Katelyn, Caitlyn, Katelynn, Katlyn, Katelin, Enid, Precious, Paris, Latrice, Shatreece, Leaisha, Cheyenne, Janeliss, Tevon, Latanya, Symphony, Clement, Jaqua, Howie, Paige, Siraya, Raycon, Kadeja, Tequella, Peddy, Nafali, Dual, Obriganna, Casmir, Martel, Sadie, Pasha, Yome, Baltimere, Taya, Oxana, Dontae, Reo, Talia, & Balen. We also could add Mattel's Flava Dolls, Happy D., Kiyoni, P. Bo, Tika, Liam and Tre.

.

The phrase "Sticks and stones will break my bones, but names will never hurt me," must have been coined by someone who never had to endure the hurtfulness and ridicule of being called a demeaning or derogatory name. In reality, your name often determines your fate – or at least the expectations have of you!

"A Boy Named Sue," a country hit from years ago, has Johnny Cash realizing that his dad purposefully gave him a girl's name because his father knew he would not be around to help the boy grow up to be big and strong. Because of what others tend to think (expect), his father knew that any boy named Sue would have to be tough in order to overcome the hostile treatment that such a name for a male would elicit. If you recall, though, Johnny Cash ends his song by declaring that he would *never* name his son Sue!

This song simply reflects real life – then and now. One's name often carries with it a stereotype; it establishes a set of expectations that others have for someone with that particular name. What pictures (set of expectations) come to mind when you think of a boy named Clyde, Elmer, Harold, Irving, Leo, Rufus, or Wallace, or a girl named Bertha, Estelle, Gertrude, Gladys, Isidore, Louise, Nellie, or Sydonie? Contrast the pictures you have of these children with the visions conjured up for boys named David, John, Richard, and Michael (some of the most popular male names in America), or girls named Anne, Jennifer, Kimberly, and Rebecca.

All other things being equal, do children's given names make any difference in the expectations that teachers hold for students' behavior, ability, and achievement? The answer is "yes." The answer is so unequivocally "yes" that we named our son, David and our daughter, Rebecca.

Although my wife and I liked the name David, we also knew that this name conjures up visions of "an achiever," "an undeniable winner, a scholar" and a "beloved one." It is a "solid," "handsome" and "strong" name. Think King David! Our daughter's name, Rebecca, summons up similar positive visions – at least for white, middle-class teachers. This is, in fact, just the image we wanted to create in the eyes of our children's beholders – their teachers. Of course, having a scholarly name does not guarantee academic success – but it can't hurt!

Your author realizes that the world is not static and that the positive expectations teachers held for our son, David, and our daughter, Rebecca, in the mid-seventies and through the eighties may not hold true, today. Other names may have superseded them. But the fact is that while they were in school and receptive to teacher expectations, the payoff of those two names was positive.

Any student of history knows that many Eastern and Southern European families who immigrated to the United States around the turn of the 20th century Americanized their names. They were aware of the stigma, the negative expectations, that commonly was associated with their "old country" original names.

Movie stars have long realized the impact names can have on their popularity with an audience. Would you rush out to view a movie with a star named Marion Morrison or Thomas C. Mapother IV? Probably not. That is why John Wayne and Tom Cruise, respectively, changed their stage name – the name that the public uses to judge their worth. Would you put down good money to view a film starring Oscar and Emmy wining Ilyena Lydia Vasilievna Mironov? I bet not. This actually is the given name of actress Dame Helen Mirren! A good name, a strong name, or a powerful name can make the difference between recognition, fame and fortune or obscurity and poverty.

What happens if you are not born with an engaging name? No problem. Change it. Here are some other actors' and actresses' stage names and their given names.

Michael Caine………..Maurice Micklewhite
Hulk Hogan…………..Terry Jean Bollette
Kirk Douglas………….Issur Danielovitch Demsky
Dame Helen Mirren…..Ilyena Lydia Vasilievna Mironov
Cary Grant…………….Archibald Alexander Leach
Lady Gaga…………….Stefanbi Angelina Germanotta
Elton John…………….Reginald Kenneth Dwight

"What's in a name?" The answer is often "everything!" Because names or titles are often the first thing we know about someone or something, they demand our attention. They are something directly under our control. Why not take advantage of it even if the advantage is slight? If you were a player in a Las Vegas casino, you would more likely be a winner if you had even a "slight advantage" over that of the house.

I am not suggesting that you change your name in order to secure more positive expectations from others. This example is simply to show the power behind "what's in a name or title." You don't need to change your name, but if you were a presenter you might decide to liven up the title of your offering – talk, lecture, spiel – now that you see its impact on expectations.

For contrast purposes, here is a selection of accurate, but a bit on the bland side, presentation titles from a recent medical conference. Do they "grab" you? Do they suggest high expectations to the attendees? Probably not.

- Osteoporosis for the Gynecologist
- Adnexal Masses: The Guidelines Have Changed
- SERMs and SPRMs: What's Now? What's Next?
- Update on Management of Spine Diseases
- CT Angiography: What's New

Here are just a few more creative titles contributed by Rebecca Sivarajah, MD. All of them are real. You might shoot for presentation titles (e.g., names) that are a little more engaging than those above and maybe a little less cutesy than those below. You decide. Your title would be your attempt at forming positive expectations.

- Chickens prefer beautiful humans.
- 5 TIWIKLY things I wish I knew last year.
- Jump performances of dog and cat fleas.
- Sword swallowing and its side effects.
- Pressures produced when penguins pooh.

With their Americanized names and the passage of a generation or two, complete with public schooling that tended to dismiss the ways of the old country, these immigrants looked (at least sounded) as if their ancestors could have come across the Atlantic with the Puritans. What's in a name? Possibly everything!

What can you expect from a name? When Japanese sports cars first came into the States, Datsun (now called Nissan) imported and named its contender *Fair Lady*. This was a bad choice, a really bad choice. It had to compete with European cars that had "racy" sounding names such as

MG, *TR-6*, *BMW* and *JAG*. And, at the time, the United States was offering muscle cars with names such as *GTO*, *Barracuda*, and *BOSS Mustang*. What chance did a sport car called *Fair Lady* have? Not much. What's in a name? A lot!

Research confirms that certain social handicaps are thrust upon the child who carries a socially undesirable name. Because there has emerged a general tendency toward negative evaluation of infrequently encountered names, a parent might think twice before naming his or her offspring for Great Aunt Gladys.

In an often-used format for testing the effect of name stereotypes on teachers' expectations, researchers have asked experienced teachers to evaluate student assignments, often consisting of short essays that have been written by students. Randomly assigned common (popular) and uncommon (unpopular) names are placed on these essays as the authors.

Do students' names make any difference in the teachers' evaluations? For teachers, the effect of the author's name upon the score assigned the essay has been shown to be significant for boys and girls. It is no coincidence that the boy's name David was the one name associated with the essay scoring the highest average.

When White, Black, and Hispanic teachers were asked to rate their impressions of typical student first names, the results indicated that raters across all three ethnic groups exhibited likes and dislikes for student first names. For male names, David, Michael, Robert, and Steven, were rated positively by all ethnic groups. The names Harold and Stanley, on the other hand, were viewed positively by Black teachers, but connoted inactivity, badness, and femininity in the judgment of Hispanic and White teachers.

Recent research identifies that it is possible to "predict," still one more word for "expect," that boys with names such as Ernest, Garland, Kareem, Malcolm, Preston, Tyrell and even the Biblical name, Luke, will be more frequently referred to the juvenile-justice system. Other research by David Figlio reports that boys with names commonly given girls are more likely to be suspended from school. He also reports that parents with less schooling are more likely to pick unpopular (at least unpopular to the ears of middle-class, primarily white, teachers) names for their children.

Consider names such as La-dasha (pronounced Ladasha). Note the actual "dash" in the name. Note the name Orangejello (basically spelled orange jello, but pronounced O rang a lo). Note the name Bidet – sounding very French, very feminine, and if one knows bathroom conveniences, very much a device for washing one's…..! Well, you know. Note the name Shithead (pronounced Sheath e add). Unfortunately, when one spells out the name, say starting with the first four letters, one encounters a problem or two. Note the name Randy (my brother's name). A fine name for the U.S., but a disastrous name for a boy or girl in Great Britain – means being sexually….!

I suppose that if you are rich and famous and your children go to school with other rich and famous people, then you probably have more latitude on selecting unusual children's names. It will never be a problem for Julia Robert's twins, Hazel and Phinnaeus. If you don't happen to be rich and famous, you can always hire a "nameologist" who, for several hundred dollars, will help you make the right choice for your son or daughter.

It may not be that unusual names *cause* problems, but having an unusual name may lead to unfavorable reactions from others which, in turn, leads to unfavorable evaluations of the self. From here the downhill spiral continues.

In other studies where elementary teachers rated male elementary students with desirable or undesirable first names on self-concept and school achievement measures, it has been found that the desirable name group differed from the other group on, among other characteristics, expectations and aspirations about behavior and achievement scores. Although most teachers may believe that their expectations are not influenced by a child's name, there is sufficient evidence indicating that name stereotyping is one aspect of expectancy behavior.

Are you able to see immediate leadership qualities in a girl named Candy or a boy named Rufus? Can you easily picture a quick-witted high school football quarterback named Cecil or Elmer, or does a Joe, John, Jack, Kirk, or Scott fit the quarterback picture better? Does a girl named Barbie best fit your image of the captain of the debate team, or do you instead immediately wonder who the Ken is in this Barbie's life? Do children named after popular perfumes of the day make you wonder just what were parents thinking when they named their offspring?

What were some parents thinking when they named their child? In New Zealand the state can step in and nix a name. For instance they said "no" to parents trying to name their child "Mafia No Fear," "Lucifer," "Fish and Chips," or "Queen Victoria. It seems that some parents, lacking a bit of inspiration, simply tried to opt for the names "2nd," "3rd," and "4th. The two funniest, but probably not all that funny for the children, were the names "Keenan Got Lucie" and "Number 16 Bus Shelter!" I suppose this shelter held "special" memories for the parents. I would like to have seen the faces on the children's teachers when they read the new class roster!

Other state outlawed names for children include, Germany says "no" to "Osama Bin Laden," Denmark says "no" to "Monkey," Saudi Arabia says "no" to "Linda," [too western], Japan says "no" to Akuma (devil)," Mexico says "no" to "Robocop" and "Circumcision," China says "no" to symbols "@," and France says "no" to "Nutella" In a protest to name restrictions, two New Zealand parents tried, unsuccessfully, to name their child what they claimed was a "noble   name," BRFXXCCXXMNPCCCCLLLMMNPRXVCLMNCKSS QLBB11116 – pronounced "Albin." I am sure that the child's teachers would have been relieved!

Keep in mind that one of the first things that teachers learn about students, even before they personally meet them, is their names. If first impressions are lasting impressions, then how teachers respond to students' names can be critical. David Figlio, a researcher at the University of Florida, reported that up to 15% of the achievement gap between black-and-white test scores may be connected to one's given name. This is staggering if even only partially correct! He further reports that lower socio-economic families assign children's names with certain suffixes such as "isha" and "ious" (think Precious as a name), included an apostrophe, or were particularly long. One can only wonder what impact these names have on the initial expectations of our primarily white, middle-class teachers. Yes, the color of today's classroom teachers is changing from mostly white to a diversity of colors. But what is not changing is the middle-class beliefs and prejudices these teachers hold.

What can you do to help your child?

- Be careful what you name your child. For instance, there was one case where parents wanted to name their child, Bidet, not knowing that the dictionary defines "bidet" as: a fixture about the height of the seat of a chair used for bathing external genitals and the posterior parts of the body!

- Make sure that your child can correctly pronounce and spell his/her given and surname.

- Allow your child the opportunity to choose whether to use first name only, first and middle names, middle name only, or initials in some combination. For instance, C. M. Charles is actually a respected *male* author of discipline books whose first name is really Carol. One wonders what playground teasing he received while in school because of his name.

- When your child enters the adult world of work, consider having him or her use first and middle initials to mask both unusual names and indications of gender (especially for females).

Add your own ideas!

- _____
- _____
- _____
- _____
- _____
- _____

A personal comment

A line delivered by Jerry Seinfeld in the situation comedy, *Seinfeld*, went something like this. "What? They named their boy, Jeeves? Now just what do you suppose this kid will grow up to be?" The audience laughs because they, like Jerry, "expect" that the infant was destined to grow up to be a butler as in "Jeeves, the butler!"

DIALECT

"I have the map of Dixie on my tongue."
(Zora Neale Hurston, Writer and Folklorist)

"Quick, let's *red* up the house before the guests come."
Pittsburgh talk for hide all of the mess.

"It's bean an ouwah since Ted lift."
Boston translation: "It has been an hour since Ted left."

A while ago I spent a year on sabbatical at Durham University in England. Northern England, in contrast to more popular tourist areas near London, is a very friendly place. My family and I were immediately accepted into the community, regularly invited into neighbors' homes, and frequently entertained by friends in local pubs.

John, a policeman, and Bob, a fireman, lived next door with their wives, Eileen and Lynn, respectively. John and Bob both spoke with a strong "Geordie" accent, characteristic of lifelong natives of this area. In a normal conversation, when, on my behalf, they slowed down their speech, I could understand them pretty well. But, when we went out to a pub and had had a pint or two, they spoke at their normal speed, and I could not understand a single word they said. Although their language definitely pegged them as being Geordies, it mattered little because neither man had any desire to travel outside of northern England.

If one really wants to "make it" in England, meaning securing one of the better (higher paying) jobs in government, in the professions, or in the worlds of finance and business, which are centered around the hub of London, one cannot have a Geordie accent. The good London-based jobs are taken by people who can speak English as they do on BBC (British Broadcasting Corporation) television. Anyone who does not speak the BBC way is instantly pegged as second class – something very important in a class-oriented society.

During my sabbatical year, the dialect problem for young high school graduates affected the schools of Scotland, the border of which was only 50 miles north of our home. Ironically, the problem was reported in documentaries on the London-based BBC-1 and BBC-2 television stations, by newscasters speaking the BBC way.

The problem surfaced as an outgrowth of the fact that so much of the industry (mining, automobile manufacturing, shipbuilding, drilling for North Sea oil) in northern England and Scotland has fallen on hard times or disappeared completely, so that there were few jobs for school leavers (high school graduates).

Although Scottish school leavers could travel to London in search of the good jobs, the minute they opened their mouths in a job interview, it would be obvious that they did not speak the preferred BBC version of the King's English. They would sound like and be judged in the same way as we might judge hillbillies who were applying for a job in the financial district of New York.

The dialect and/or primary language issue has also emerged as our nation and our nation's schools struggle with the dilemma of how much to impose Standard English on our citizens. The facts are indisputable: As groups, African Americans, Hispanic Americans, and other second dialect speakers consistently underachieve academically, and children in states with a large proportion of second dialect speakers do poorly on national standardized examinations. Are many of these students who speak a non-standard English hurt by teachers' pejorative attitudes (e.g., negative expectations) regarding the children's dialect?

Closer to home – in fact, across the hall from me when I was still teaching – a young history professor colleague of mine who had a strong west Texas drawl to his speech confessed that when he presented professional papers at national conferences the audience's initial reaction was, "Who is this country-sounding bumpkin?" He had to proceed well into the spirited delivery of his well-researched and strongly defended argument before the audience looked beyond his speech and paid attention to his message.

No doubt, Standard English is the prestige dialect of the United States. Not the least of its value is the Pygmalion effect whereby teachers tend to rate students by their speech characteristics. Think of Eliza Doolittle in the play, *My Fair Lady*. As you may recall, she could not truly become a princess until she "spoke" and acted like one – hence, Professor's Higgins "The rain in Spain falls mostly in the plain" training for Eliza. Higgins claimed that simple phonetics, how someone spoke, allowed him to deduce a person's origins to within a six-mile radius in London. That somewhere could be the East End, or it could be Kensington or Chelsea. A "princess" would not be expected to be from the East End.

In studies where randomly assigned teachers listened to Black Dialect-speaking children and to Standard English-speaking children respond to a series of questions, a clear winner emerged. Specifically, teachers were asked what they thought were the chances of the child's successfully finishing second grade, what the IQ of the student was, and how well the child was performing in reading.

Results revealed that teachers expected significantly greater overall academic achievement, intelligence, and reading success from those children who spoke Standard English than from those who spoke Black Dialect. The reader is reminded that these teachers' expectations were formed after listening to students speak on an audiotape for only five minutes.

It could be said that speaking Black English rather than Standard English will forever brand students as outsiders, even long after they have graduated. Children who continue to speak anything other than more standard English do so at their own peril. More standard English is the "cash language" in America, the language of the powerful, the language others listen to!

The moment children open their mouths to speak, it is clear to some (including teachers) whether or not these children are culturally literate. Once these first impressions have been formed, the almost irreversible self-fulfilling prophecy process is triggered. The lack of skill in the use of Standard English that a child exhibits at the beginning of his or her formal education has increasingly been recognized as a major factor in the degree of success that a child will have in school.

Even young children, themselves, recognize on some level that non-Standard English is stigmatized. When listening to adults speak, as would be the case in a classroom, children rate Standard English-speaking adults as smart, pretty, rich, and nice. They rate non-Standard English-speaking adults as dumb, ugly, poor, and mean.

It can be argued that poor English is *not* the language of our schools, it is *not* the language on the SAT or GRE, and it is *not* the language of better-paying jobs. But it an almost sure path to a minimum-wage job (Source unknown). Bill Cosby received some angry elitist criticisms when talking about the some inner-city dialects when he said, "I can't even talk the way these people talk, 'Why you ain't' 'Where you is' and I blamed the kid until I heard the mother and dad talk. "You can't be a doctor with that kind of crap coming out of your mouth."

Although it may be true that one's language can and should be appreciated for its uniqueness, and one can be proud of an accent or dialect, some, such as a group in Kentucky, argue that there are times that it must be lost (or at least put aside) – especially if you want to work professionally. You decide.

What can you do to help your child?

- To be forewarned is to be forearmed! Parents need to be aware that their child's minority dialect will probably be judged less favorably by middle class teachers – white, black, or Hispanic.

- Without losing any part of one's culture, consider helping your child to learn, *and to use*, standard English in school and work settings. In effect, your child would be bilingual. This could be a real positive expectations factor both in school, and later, at work.

- Be sure that your child does well on school assignments that do not require verbalization on their part (term papers, projects, leaf collections, etc.). These non-verbalization assignments can help your child form positive expectations in the minds of his or her teachers.

- Expose your child regularly to standard English by encouraging him/her to watch national news programs and the local Public Broadcasting Station. Normally these prime-time newscasters, whether NBC's Lester Holt, or a variety of BBC announcers, use the kind of standard English that one may wish to emulate.

Add your own ideas!

- _____
- _____
- _____
- _____
- _____

GENDER

"One is not born a woman, one becomes one."
(Simone de Beauvoir, *Le Deuxieme Sexe*)

Boys will be boys, girls will be girls, and the late French singer, Maurice Chevalier, applauds the differences. But what are the differences between girls and boys? From childhood we learn that "girls are made of sugar and spice and everything nice," while "boys are made of snakes and snails and puppy dog tails."

What truth is there to this contrasting description of girls and boys? The fact is, there does not have to be any real truth to the description at all. All that is important is that parents, teachers, or others *believe* the contrasting descriptions. These *beliefs*, alone, will trigger contrasting expectations of girls and boys and, in turn, will trigger contrasting (differential) behaviors towards them.

From the moment of birth, infant boys and girls are treated differently. Girls are dressed in pink; boys are dressed in blue. Girls wear little, frilly, lace-trimmed dresses, hardly conducive to active play. Boys wear jeans and other durable clothes designed to withstand active play. We hold and cuddle girls, we tease and roughhouse with boys. Girls are soothed and comforted when experiencing pain. Boys are told to handle pain by "acting like a man" (e.g., when getting a shot at the doctor's office or falling off a tricycle).

Girls are given so-called girl-appropriate toys, and boys are given so-called boy-appropriate toys. If you don't know which toys are which, simply visit your local chain toy store. The boys' toys will be in one section, and the girls' toys will be in another section. When asked why the toys are separated, toy store representatives respond by saying, "We are just arranging the toys the way the public wants."

In preparation for female adulthood, girls are encouraged to role-play a limited number of often caring-oriented careers such as nurse, teacher, mother, and housewife. In preparation for male adulthood, boys are encouraged to role-play more active, often more respected, and higher-paying careers such as policeman, doctor, lawyer, scientist, and engineer.

To the extent that the nurturing (nature vs. nurture) of children contributes to what kind of adults they will grow up to be, how they are treated as children makes a great deal of difference. Adults' expectations of what girls and boys *can* and *should* do trigger the adults' differential behaviors towards these boys and girls. The effect of these differential behaviors is felt for a lifetime.

Self-fulfilling prophecy research mirrors real-life SFP experience. For instance, in the study of "wait-time," the amount of time teachers allow before providing the correct answer or calling on another student, it has been found that elementary teachers provided significantly more wait-time for male than for female students. Providing a longer wait-time for boys in mathematics classes, for instance, conveys to them that the teacher expects that they know the answers. Calling upon boys more often also conveys to boys that they had better be prepared because the odds are, they will be called upon.

Science teachers, too, appear to treat boys and girls differently. Apparently, teachers, consciously or subconsciously, provide differential educational treatment to boys and girls during science, resulting in the failure of girls to develop their scientific abilities sufficiently. Gender-based differential teacher behaviors include female students' being called upon, praised, and criticized less often than male students, and rarely asked to give a scientific demonstration or to manipulate scientific equipment.

What makes matters even worse is the fact that elementary teachers who hold higher scientific expectations for boys are, themselves, more likely to be female. One can only wonder at the negative impact upon female students of observing female teachers exhibiting higher expectations for male students.

Ongoing research supports the fact that teachers interact with male students more often than they do female students in ways likely to convey positive expectations. The title of a book by Sadker and Sadker, *Failing at Fairness: How Our Schools Cheat Girls*, states the position well. Some of the paragraph headings of this book are "Pretty Is – Handsome Does" (it is clear who the doers are),

"Silent Losses" (guess who is more silent, males or females), and "Out of Sight, Out of Mind" (guess which gender is slighted in the curriculum no matter the subject area). These headings point out how gender-dependent a child's education is in our nation's schools.

If school is, in part, a preparation for the adult world of work, what effect does a student's gender have on a teacher's prediction of an occupation for that student? When researchers asked a group of teachers to assess what level of occupation they expected a large group of third grade and sixth grade students to achieve as adults, a clear gender bias emerged. Apparently, sex bias is present in teachers' occupational expectations for their students. Males were expected to enter unskilled, skilled and managerial occupations, while females were expected to hold lower paying and lower status, gender traditional clerical positions.

Many professional societies have their members use only initials for their given name and/or middle name, thus concealing the gender of the author. Why is this so important? Researchers had college students rate, on a scale of 1 (highly favored) to 5 (highly unfavored), an article with respect to the value of the article, its intellectual depth, the competence of the author, and the quality of the article.

The articles, from various disciplines, carried one of several author names: John T. McKay, Joan T. McKay, J. T. McKay, Chris T. McKay, or no name (unauthored). Researchers found that when reviewers assumed that the article was written by a male (e.g., John T.), they rated it higher than if they thought it had been written by a female (e.g., Joan T.). This "pro-male" bias held even when the articles were supposedly from a feminine-dominated field (e.g., psychology of women).

What can you do to help your child?

- *Read, read, read* stories to your child about heroes and heroines reflecting the child's gender. Many of these people, especially heroines, may not regularly appear in a school's curriculum.

- See if your child's school has a plan or policy of adding curriculum materials that are more gender balanced – e.g., female characters in stories shown to be as able to solve problems as their male counterparts.

- Volunteer to serve on school committees that have some say-so in selecting library books, reading materials, etc., to help insure that they are gender balanced.

- Arrange for your child to meet successful people of your child's gender who work in a variety of careers – especially those representing careers that the child might not regularly come in contact with – e.g., female tool and die worker or surgeon, and male nurse or kindergarten teacher. Folks are flattered to share their life-long career passion with a child.

- When discussing career opportunities with your child, avoid using labels like "male nurse" or "woman doctor" that subtly convey these roles as abnormal.

- Allow your children to watch appropriate television programs in which persons of their gender are positively portrayed and no gender stereotype is evident.

- Discuss with your children examples of tasks and/or jobs that are done by males or females. Point out that it does not matter if one if male or female, but how well the job or task is done.

- Resist assigning household chores on the basis of traditional stereotypic roles for males and females. Boys can cook, clean and set the table; girls can wash cars, mow the yard and take out the trash.

- If a preschool is available for your child, choose one that provides a gender-neutral learning environment. A Montessori school, for instance, provides children with didactic materials (apparatus designed to teach) that are completely gender neutral.

Add your own ideas!

- _____
- _____
- _____
- _____
- _____
- _____

Note: Many of the suggestions offered for "Gender" will be repeated under the expectation-triggering factors of "Race" and "Ethnicity."

A personal comment!

A colleague of mine, one of the most gender-neutral in attitude persons I have ever known, just yesterday showed me pictures of her first grandchild – a boy. She was beaming with pride! One of the pictures showed a gift her college-age son (the newborn's uncle) had bought him. It was a big, shiny, metal steam shovel! I just wonder what the gift would have been if the newborn had been a girl? I'll bet the gift would not have been a steam shovel!

Another personal comment!

Just this afternoon I visited with the director of a local preschool. While chatting with her (believe it or not, on the subject of "expectations"), a young girl came in to give the director a hug and say goodbye for the afternoon. The child was holding an action figure of some sort. The director said to her aide, "Why don't you see if we have something more suitable for a girl!" I assume that she believed that actions figures were inappropriate for little girls. Do you?

"It's important to remember that feminism is no longer a group of organizations or leaders. It's the expectations that parents have for their daughters, and their sons, too."
(Anna Quindlen)

BODY BUILD & WEIGHT

"If anything is sacred the human body is sacred."
(Walt Whitman, *I Sing Body Electric*)

Like it or not, society tells us – often behind our backs – that certain body builds are preferable to others. People with one type of body build are destined to lead; people with other types of body builds are destined to follow, and that's just the way it is!

In a walk down nostalgia lane, you might recall that in the western, *Wild Bill Hickok*, the handsome hero had the good build; his sidekick, Jingles (not the most manly of names), played by Andy Devine, was overweight and could be heard at the end of each program screaming in a shrill, raspy voice, "Wait for me, Wild Bill," as Wild Bill quickly and easily outdistanced his portly partner.

On *The Andy Griffith Show*, a show that has held its popularity across generations, Andy Taylor is the well-built sheriff, the person in charge. Barney Fife, the deputy sheriff who could not even be trusted with bullets in his gun, was played by skinny-as-a-rail Don Knotts, who was, at best, inept and hyperactive. Don Knotts's character changed little when he later played the easily fooled landlord on *Three's Company*.

Can overweight people be the stars? Can skinny people be the stars? Sure, they can, but most often in comedies – Jackie Gleason (*Jackie Gleason Show*) and Drew Carey, as well as his outrageously dressed, overweight secretary (*Drew Carey Show*). Overweight, as well as skinny, people can be stars, but normally only when well-built people are missing from the cast.

For instance, television networks' morning program anchors, a high-status position, whether male or female, have an average build. The lower status position of weatherman, on the other hand, as on NBC's "Today Show," is held by, until gastric bypass surgery, an overweight Al Roker.

Is there a pattern here that is based upon body build? More important in regard to the message of this book, is life really like this in the classroom? Yes, too often it is! Although people may gain and lose weight as they grow older, their basic body build normally remains the same. Body builds can be categorized into three general types or somatotypes – endomorphic, mesomorphic, & ectomorphic.

Endomorphs have round, soft bodies, with a central concentration of mass. Less tactful descriptions might be that these people are "heavy," "chubby," "plump," "stout," and even "fat." Jerry Seinfeld's stocky sidekick, George, would be classified as an endomorph. Jerry's pain-in-the-side neighbor, Neuman, also is an endomorph. Endomorphs are viewed as social but not socially assertive, even-tempered, humorous, and trusting – maybe even gullible. Extreme endomorphs are considered less attractive and often are discriminated against or stigmatized.

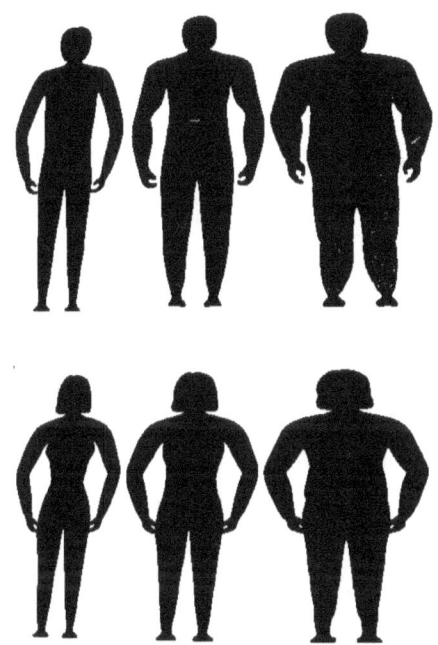

Mesomorphs have square, rugged shoulders, small buttocks, and bodies with conspicuous muscles. George Clooney from the *ER* show, and Andy Griffith from *The Andy Griffith Show* would be described as mesomorphs. Mesomorphs are seen as being aggressive, socially assertive, strong, independent, energetic, good-looking, competitive and good at physical activities. Mesomorphs, in effect, have the ideal American body build.

Ectomorphs have thin, fragile-looking bodies, drooping shoulders, and elongated, forward-bent necks. Don Knotts, who played the deputy sheriff on *The Andy*

Griffith Show, would typify an ectomorph. Ectomorphs are judged as being pessimistic, uncompetitive, sensitive, in need of friends, underconfident, inhibited, and nervous.

When approximately 50 subjects in an experiment were shown the three male body types above (where race, and ethnicity, etc. were concealed), their responses were shocking. The subjects' responses always favored the mesomorph build!

Needless to say, mesomorphs have the edge in all categories. Don't you just find the responses to #10, in particular, outrageous? How could body build determine who is and is not a good or poor father?

Sample responses follow.

Somatotypes (body builds)		
Endo	Meso	Ecto

1. Would assume leadership?

5	42	3

2. Would eat the least?

4	4	42

3. Have many friends?

16	30	4

4. Be the poorest athlete?

37	0	13

5. Be least preferred as a friend?

22	9	19

6. Would endure pain the best?

10	30	10

7. Smokes 3 packs of cigarettes a day?

15	7	28

8. Would make the poorest doctor?

19	9	22

9. Would least likely be chosen leader?

25	10	15

10. Would make the poorest father?

19	7	24

There is little doubt that personality factors are associated with these three body types. A child's personality, once allowed to be influenced by the expectations of others, can bias how he or she acts toward those who held the original expectations. It is not then, just that others expect people, including children, with certain body builds to act a certain way. The people, themselves, eventually expect themselves to act that way.

When do body build stereotypes begin to form in young children? When researchers asked kindergarten through fourth-grade students to rate line drawings of thin, average, and chubby body types on pairs of bipolar adjectives (e.g., brave/afraid, smart/stupid, strong/weak), predictable results emerged. The average-build child (line drawing) was perceived as favorable, while the chubby-build child (line drawing) was seen as unfavorable. The thin-build child (line drawing) emerged as a combination of the socially desirable traits identified with the average-build stereotype and the negative physical capability traits associated with the chubby-build stereotype.

Other studies have found a clear association between the good occupations, the prestigious occupations, and one body build – mesomorph! Mesomorphic body builds were associated with such careers as stock broker, manager of a large factory, electrical engineer, and superintendent of schools. Ectomorphs were associated with accountant, bookkeeper, typist, and file clerk. Endomorphs were associated with garbage collector, butcher, janitor, and restaurant pastry chef.

Still other studies show that when elementary and middle school students are presented with female silhouettes representing endomorph, mesomorph, and ectomorph body builds and then asked to assign a series of behavior/personality trait adjectives to them, a clear winner emerges. Mesomorphs are described as strong, best friend, clean, happy, polite, honest, brave, good-looking, smart, and neat. Ectomorphs are described as quiet, worried, nervous, sick, sneaky, afraid, sad, and weak. Endomorphs are described as cheats, people who argue, lie, get teased and as lazy, dirty, and stupid. There clearly is a stereotypic pattern for the three female body images within age levels and across age levels. The mesomorphic image is perceived as entirely favorable.

Several states are instituting laws that will make it a serious crime for students in school to taunt, bully, or otherwise harass other students including doing such things as slapping a sign on a child's back saying "hippo," "fatty," or other such demeaning messages. Schools have an obligation to monitor such behavior because it can create an unhealthy learning environment. Ignoring the issue can have serious consequences. Recently, an overweight child could not take the constant derogatory comments of his school peers regarding his weight. He took his father's gun and killed himself!

"Wait, wait….Don't Tell Me"
(*National Public Radio*)

When one actually reads the quotation, above, it is clear that we are talking about the popular *NPR* weekly news-based radio program where panelists answer questions. But, if you were to simply "hear" the quotation, you might assume it is saying, "Weight…Weight. Don't Tell Me." You might think that there are those who just do not want to know the lower expectations that often accompany overweight people no matter their age.

Study after study shows that teachers (and others) discriminate against obese students as early as elementary school. Although most of us know that this is the case, what we might not know is that obesity may contribute to lower academic success of overweight girls, especially in feminine preferred classes such as English. Less discrimination for these same girls occurs in math and science classes.

To some, we have a which came first, the "chicken or the egg" situation. Do fatter kids simply under-perform in school and, hence, the teachers simply report what they observe? Or, do the negative expectations some teachers hold for overweight students contribute to kids' lower performance? Overall, the discriminatory (e.g., lower expectations) impact of being overweight appears to strike females more than males.

It appears that obesity (versus race, religion and gender) is the last socially acceptable form of bias (e.g., negative expectations). Seriously overweight children are ripe as targets for bullying whether it is physical or social. One overweight person lamented that people around her regularly make "snap judgments" because of her overweight appearance. This just goes to reinforce how quickly an expectation, high or low, can be assigned to a child by a teacher.

What can you do to help your child?

- Control your child's diet, and stress good nutrition. Better still, model a good diet and proper nutrition for them.

- Encourage your child to exercise. Better still, model it for them; exercise as a family.

- Choose your child's clothing carefully, selecting those clothes that are more flattering. (Call a local fashion consultant – often located at a nearby shopping mall to seek advice.)

- Help your child select magazines that present models who better represent the real world's wide range of body builds rather than the unrealistic fashion models held up for display.

- Pay attention to information regarding the staggering increase in obesity among children. For whatever reason, children in the United State, more so than any other industrialized country, are now categorized as obese. The impact on children's health is well documented and openly discussed. The impact of obesity on a child's life opportunities (e.g., career choices) is not so well known. And, if known, are not openly discussed.

- Tell your child, and continue to reinforce the fact, that in spite of many peoples' initial negative expectations of overweight, as well as skinny children, these people's (e.g., teachers') minds can be changed by stressing one's positive factors, such as scholarship, good communication skills, attention to detail, neatness, dependability (e.g., regular attendance, meeting or beating assigned deadlines), manners, etc.

- Read stories to your child about heroes and heroines reflecting your child's body build. Point out in the media or other contexts where adults mirroring your child's body build are achieving. Many of these people may not regularly appear in a school's curriculum.

- Check with your child's school to see whether or not they have a policy regarding the taunting, bullying, and/or otherwise harassing of students by peers (and teachers). If there is no policy, consider asking that one be formed. If there is a policy, get a copy of it and ask that it be enforced.

- Encourage your child to participate in activities (sports and otherwise) at a young age so that he or she can gain more positive feelings about himself or herself. These positive feelings may help combat some negative expectations regarding weight that may be directed towards him or her when entering school. This early participation in activities also can solidify lifelong friendships that look beyond body build and other expectation-triggering factors.

- Be aware that though it may appear sexist and unfair, there is a link between absent mothers (mothers who have to, or choose to, work) and overweight children. Unsupervised children, home after school, are choosing their own snacks – and making bad choices.

For your information: Who is standing next to you?

A recent news item cited research that showed that people of average builds who even stand next to overweight or obese people are judged, themselves, as less desirable – just like the overweight or obese person. I suppose observers feel "birds of a feather flock together." I know it is not fair. You know it is not fair. Everyone knows that it is not fair. But it happens.

For your Information: Financial Impact of Obesity

Volumes could be written on the negative impact of obesity. Here is one financial example. It is reported that obesity can mean less pay. Paychecks of obese workers are, on average, about 2.5% less than their thinner counterparts in the same professions. And the wage penalty is much greater for overweight women – as much as 6.2%." In dollars and cents this could mean more than a $2,500 to $3,500 difference in a yearly salary for an overweight person.

Companies realize that obese individuals tend to be sicker, miss work more often, have lower productivity, and tend to inflate health care costs. In schools, obese children miss more school days than normal weight children, generally display more emotional difficulties, exhibit lower performance, and are less socially adept. All of these factors influence teachers' expectations.

For your information: Putting on / taking off "weight"

Did you happen to see the *ABC*, October 27, 2003, television program titled "Fat like me: How to win the weight war?" It featured a teenage girl, Ali Schmidt, who dressed up in a "fat suit," complete with facial makeup and tent-like clothes to accent her "weight." In reality, Ali was a tall, thin, athletic girl who volunteered to attend a new school for a day and have video-taped the reactions of her peers and teachers to her "weight." You can imagine the terrible and hurtful looks, stares, and comments she endured.

Actually, those of us who are not significantly overweight probably cannot imagine how overweight kids feel every day. The program was painful even to watch. Ali returned to the same school the next day after having taken off all of her "weight." Gee, if it were just that easy for overweight people. A moderator, Ali, and selected students then discussed what had transpired the day before.

Add your own ideas!

- _____
- _____
- _____
- _____
- _____

ATTRACTIVENESS

"Go home and tell your daughters they're beautiful."
(Stokely Carmichael, Activist)

Beauty is good; lack of beauty is bad, sometimes downright evil. From infancy, we are schooled to believe that good and bad, smart and dumb, and clean and dirty are features, respectively, associated with good-looking people and with not-so-good-looking people. In fairy tales such as *Cinderella*, read to us by loving parents, we have the handsome prince and the beautiful maiden (representing all that is good in our world), and the ugly stepmother and stepsisters (representing all that is bad). In *Sleeping Beauty*, we have a beautiful princess given a poison apple by an ugly, wart-faced witch who represents evil. Beauty suggests goodness; ugliness, of course, suggests wickedness.

In the Saturday morning cowboy serials of days past, the hero, who always won in the end, was good-looking. The bad guys were downright ugly and, to the hurrah of the audience, always lost – got caught or shot – in the end. Good guys looked like good guys, and bad guys looked like bad guys. The message that "beauty is good" or "handsome is good" and, therefore, by inference "ugliness is bad – even repulsive" continues to bombard us, both on television and in the cinema.

So, is there really a big problem? Surely everyone knows that fairy tales are just that – make-believe tales made up to entertain (sometimes scare) children. But do children learn and take with them into adulthood the "beauty is good" message from the media while they are being entertained?

What evidence is there in real life that adults, in general, act on their "beauty is good" beliefs? And more germane to the subject of this book, what evidence is there that teachers allow this "beauty is good" theory to influence their interactions with students?

To the extent that beauty is something that is in the "eye of the beholder," the beholder holds tremendous expectations-type power over the beholdee! The conditions are ripe for the self-fulfilling prophecy to operate with students either living up to or down to the Pygmalion's (e.g., teacher's) expectations.

Although beauty, as an abstract notion, is not easy to define, it may not be impossible to do so. There is more than a passing cross-cultural agreement as to those facial features generally judged to be attractive. Research shows that a good-looking face is one with regular, typical features; an ugly face is one with unwelcomed surprises.

A student's facial attractiveness is a factor in a teacher's expectations. Are they earned or are they awarded out of a sense of entitlement, but the fact is attractive people earn higher grades. What is interesting is that many good-looking people, themselves, and those around them (e.g., teachers), believe that better looking people deserve all of the benefits that they receive.

Less good looking people do not receive these same benefits. But, at least they have a newly coined term almost all to themselves – "lookism," a word to describe or define the discriminatory treatment most often delivered to physically unattractive people. It negatively impacts them at work, in romance, in job opportunities, etc.

Attractive people are more likely to be perceived more favorably. This translates into a greater willingness on the part of others to help them, more likelihood that they will be hired, a greater probability that they will be promoted, and a greater chance that they will be treated more favorably by our court systems – all because they are attractive! After all, who wouldn't want to help "good" people?

If it is any consolation, there is one area where beautiful people, especially women, lose out. They are less likely to be hired for low-level, low paying, entry-level jobs. The thought is that too soon they will be dissatisfied with their job and, because they still harbor feelings of entitlement, after all they are beautiful, they will want to move on to greener pastures leaving the position to be filled once again. The moral of this story appears to be that if you want a crappy job, don't be too good looking, and if you want a good job with great benefits, be really good looking.

For instance, on a classic and enlightening *60 Minutes* television show, two women took turns playing the role of a stranded motorist in a downtown area. One young woman, through the help of makeup, was made to look less attractive. With her car hood up, obviously in need of assistance, she stood and waited as cars just whizzed by. Occasionally someone would stop and, at most, volunteer information about where she could walk to get gasoline.

The other woman, although dressed the same and also obviously in need of assistance, was blond and, by society's standards, much more attractive. Cars came screeching to a stop, and men stumbled over each other volunteering to render assistance. In no time at all, the attractive woman had her gas tank half filled! No doubt, being attractive has its benefits.

Still another women's attorney pleaded with the judge that his defendant, Brenda LaFave, was simply too pretty to go to jail. Does it sound like a silly defense? Well, it worked. She didn't go to jail!

In another event, the website, BeautifulPeople.com "expelled" over a thousand members who, after apparently enjoying (e.g., eating) the holiday too much and gaining weight, were no longer welcome at a site that focuses upon beautiful people meeting other beautiful people. The rejected members were given an opportunity to reapply but only a few were voted back in.

Although "beauty may be only skin deep," we all know that much attention is paid to those parts of us seen by other people – especially in forming their first, sometimes their lasting, impressions. It would be naive to believe that our preoccupation with a person's beauty stops at the schoolhouse door.

Can elementary teachers predict from photographs which elementary students will have more positive peer relationships, evidence greater academic ability, and be better adjusted? The answer, according to researchers, is "Yes." Just look for the more attractive students.

In one study, researchers had teachers rate school students, first on attractiveness (photographs displayed on color slides), and second on a series of personal characteristics (e.g., confidence, sociability). The teachers' ratings of attractiveness correlated with their positive judgments of children's sociability, popularity, academic achievement, confidence, and leadership. Clearly, teachers believed that they could predict a good deal about children from simply viewing their photographs.

In another study, female Head Start preschool teachers were interviewed to determine the effects of a child's physical attractiveness on initial teacher expectations. These teachers were shown a randomly assigned photograph of one of the children (independently judged previously as being either extremely attractive or extremely unattractive) and asked to predict how they felt the child would do in their classroom if so assigned. A child's level of attractiveness was found to influence teachers' initial expectations regarding the child's behavior **and** likely school success. Implications for the well-being of children who attend early intervention preschool programs are evident.

Teachers' expectations based upon student attractiveness can eventually translate into actual academic advantages. To make matters even more unfair, it appears that teachers not only favor the attractive children, but also discriminate against the unattractive children. There also is evidence that a student's physical attractiveness influences teachers' disciplinary behavior toward students.

How old are children when they first begin to judge physical attractiveness the same way that adults do? Children begin to use similar or common criteria in judging physical attractiveness at approximately age 6 and increase thereafter until the age of 8, when they use the same criteria as older judges. It appears, then, that the kindergarten through third grades can be especially important in emphasizing the criteria one's culture uses to define attractiveness.

Some researchers have found that children's judgments, at least regarding attractive and unattractive peers, can be made even by 3- to 6-year-olds. Young children, when shown photographs, have been reported to have chosen attractive rather than unattractive children as those they would most like to have as their friends. Even infants have been observed showing a preference (e.g., smiling more, staring longer) for photographs of attractive rather than less attractive faces.

Does the "beauty is good" hypothesis hold equally for males and females? Being attractive can be an advantage for both sexes, but, while unattractive females are judged negatively in almost all cases, unattractive males are sometimes evaluated positively. If one must be unattractive, it is a better fate to be male than female.

Expectations based upon attractiveness can be a two-edged sword. Research has shown that elementary school students consistently choose attractive teachers as being the nicest people, the happiest, the ones they would learn the most from and unattractive teachers as the ones who would punish their students when they misbehaved. Children display a significant tendency to prefer attractive teachers. Thus, less attractive teachers can look forward to an uphill battle to overcome these impressions, even though they may possess obvious teaching competence.

Attractiveness is an immediately obvious human characteristic and one that adults (including teachers) seem to favor. If a child looks like a teacher's idea of an attractive student – looks, acts, and dresses the part, are they likely to show favoritism? Teachers award these attractive children higher grades, praise them more, criticize them less, discipline them less and less harshly, and so forth.

Note, I purposefully have not included my picture in this book for fear that the book's contents might be judged by my attractiveness or unattractiveness. Although we all know that "one cannot judge a book by its cover," we often do form an initial judgment of a book by the author's picture on the book jacket. Don't we?

It is a fact that students, even college and university students, will evaluate more harshly (e.g., lower) professors who are "older" and "uglier" than those who are "younger" and "better looking." While time marches on and I have steadily been getting older, when I look in the mirror, I still see a relatively good-looking man, just a bit uglier!

Because all of my university classes were evaluated by my students, I used to hold up in front of my face a mask of a handsome young soccer player from Australia. I picked it up on a vacation while there a few years ago. My thinking is that the students might be fooled into thinking that I, too, am young and handsome and, thus, will evaluate my teaching more positively. Hope spring eternal doesn't it!

What can you do to help your child?

- Play to your child's strengths. Sometimes cute and perky, or stoic and dignified, can carry the day just as much as natural beauty.

- Avoid commenting upon the physical appearance of public and celebrity figures during casual conversations with your child. (Note that both positive and negative comments indicate that appearance makes a difference in a person's job performance.)

- Provide your child's teachers and administrators with up-to-date materials (e.g., magazine and journal articles, references to upcoming or recently presented television investigations) that address the bias that exists in favor of more beautiful people. Although providing this kind of information has been offered under the factor "attractiveness," it is a suggestion that can apply to all of the factors (e.g., race, ethnicity, body-build) presented in this book.

Add your own ideas!

- _____
- _____
- _____
- _____

RACE

"You have to expect things of yourself before you can do them."
(Michael Jordan, *GQ*, March, 1989)

Justice is blind. False! Justice is not blind. Persons of color tend to receive more, as well as more intense, punishment by the nation's courts when they break society's rules than do their fellow white citizens.

Well, at least the job market is color-blind; people are hired, as well as promoted on merit alone. False! The job market is not color-blind. Persons of color tend to get hired, as well as promoted less often than do their Caucasian counterparts.

Certainly, food and housing are available equally to all American citizens who can afford them, regardless of the color of their skin. False! Restaurants that quickly serve white patrons may make persons of color wait, and apartments advertised as being available suddenly become unavailable when persons of color (or people with disabilities) make inquiries.

At least in schools, teachers as educated professionals, treat all students the same regardless of the students' race. False! Among other practices, students of color more often are placed in lower academic tracks when undeserved, as well as disciplined more and more harshly, than their white student peers.

Race is one of those distinguishing human characteristics that, unlike one's religion, ethnicity, or socioeconomic status, cannot be easily hidden from view. Thus, barring any other knowledge that you might possess about someone you see for the first time, you immediately know his or her race.

As a child growing up in a steel city where blacks and whites went to the same high school together but who often lived in separate housing areas, the one and only Black "hero" that your author was made aware of was George Washington Carver. What did he do? I was told he worked with peanuts! It wasn't until many years later that I learned that he was an educator, agriculturist, author, reformer, and performing artist. I also learned that Thomas Edison offered Carver $100,000 (a lot of money back then) per year to move to New Jersey and work in his labs. Carver refused and stayed at Tuskegee University. Wow.

Not all that long ago I viewed the video, *Gifted Hands* (played by Cuba Goodings, Jr.), the story of Dr. Benjamin S. Carson who made medical history in 1987 by performing the first successful surgery (22 hours along) when he led a 70-member medical team that separated twins conjoined at the back of the head. Carson, later a Director of Pediatric Neurosurgery at Johns Hopkins Children's Center, was a troubled African-American kid from the inner city whose father had abandoned the family leaving his uneducated mother on her own. I'll bet Carson's story is not known by a lot of today's classroom teachers. It should be. It would help create more positive expectations, first in the minds of teachers and, then, in the minds of the teachers' students!

Knowing another person's race, though, is not the problem. The problems are the expectations (bias, prejudice, predisposition) one forms based upon that person's race and the subsequent differential behaviors toward that person. Minority students are often the focus of negative teacher expectations and the corresponding negative expectation's effects.

Research shows that African Americans (as well as Mexican Americans) often are graded unfairly in public schools. At times a grade ceiling exists for minorities. In one scenario, researchers describe the experience of a Black female graduate-student. The student claimed that she had one instructor who gave her a "C" because the professor thought that most Blacks were used to getting "C's"!

What other perceptions do Black students have of their teachers' treatment of them? To answer this question, researchers inventoried a group of Black and White fifth-grade students from an affluent suburban mid-Atlantic public-school system. The bad news is that when data were analyzed by gender, Black males perceived that their teachers treated them in ways that were usually reserved for lower achieving students. Black males reported that their teachers expected less from them, called on them less, scolded them for not trying and for not listening, and gave them more negative feedback than the teachers did for Whites and for Black females. Is it any wonder that Black males drop out of school at a rate higher than any other race/gender/ethnicity group?

One aspect of education where Blacks (as well as other minorities) may be especially at risk because of teachers' expectations is in the dispensing of punishment. Do teachers punish according to race? A recent article described a large, midwestern school system's junior high "dungeon," or in-school suspension room, located adjacent to the basement boiler room. Sentenced students remain in this hot, windowless room throughout the entire day as punishment for school infractions. It was found that Black students were twice as likely to end up in the dungeon as White students. In fact, Black students were twice as likely to end up disciplined throughout the entire public-school system.

In some schools a modified caste system exists where students' academic success is predicted by teachers from the students' skin color. In such schools, teachers attribute Black students with probable underachievement due to cultural deprivation, lack of interest in school, no future goals, and lack of parental interest. Teachers need to learn more about racial and ethnic families before they form such unwarranted assumptions.

When a school's culture (e.g., teachers' culture) comes up against an urban Black culture, teachers need to set the same high academic standards and expectations for Black students (and other minorities) that they should set for all students, and then they need to hold all students strictly accountable for meeting those standards.

Otherwise, a self-fulfilling prophecy is set in motion as teachers expect Black students to fail regardless of their actual academic potential and so adjust their own behavior in ways that may help bring these expectations to fruition.

What can you do to help your child?
- See if your child's school has a plan or policy of adding curriculum materials that are more racially diverse.

- Volunteer to serve on school committees that have some say-so in selecting library books, reading materials, etc., to help insure that the offerings are balanced when it comes to race. At the same time, though, keep the focus on the task at hand. Do not use such volunteering as a pulpit for furthering personal causes.

- Arrange for your child to meet successful people of your child's race who work in a variety of careers-- especially those representing careers that the child might not regularly come in contact with. Most folks are flattered when asked to share their life-long career passion with a child.

- Encourage your child to watch appropriate television programs in which persons of their race are positively portrayed and no racial stereotype is evident.

- Discuss with your child examples and stories that reflect proud moments associated with one's racial background, in general, and with one's family, in particular. When your child enters school, he or she may well have opportunities to share--with pride--some of these stories with his or her classmates.

- *Read, read, read* stories to your child about heroes and heroines reflecting the child's race. Many of these people, authors, engineers, mathematicians, chemists, etc., may not regularly appear in a school's curriculum. Use the Internet, or any other source, to identify Black heroes and heroines. A quick click on most of these names (found on the Internet) quickly brings up a biographical sketch. If no Internet service exists at home, use the Internet services found free of charge at most local public libraries. Encourage your child to research these individuals. Better still, join them in this research. A *partial list* of Black, and in the next chapter, Hispanic heroes and heroines follow.

Add to these two collections still other popular Black and Hispanic musicians, actors and actresses, sportspeople, politicians, scientists, and medical personnel, and the lists would be much, much longer!

Add your own ideas!
- _____
- _____
- _____
- _____
- _____
- _____

BLACK HEROES / HEROINES

Among your author's personal favorites are Pearl Bailey, Thurgood Marshall (1st Black Supreme Court Justice), Rosa Parks (1st women to lie in State in the Capitol Rotunda), and Rod Paige (once held the position of Secretary of Education for the United States). My wife's favorites would include Tiger Woods!

Others include, Angela Davis, Zora Neale Hurston, Toni Morrison, Alice Walker, Ida B. Wells-Barnett, Phillis Wheatley, Maya Angelou, Rita Dove, Harriet Jacobs, Jamaica Kincaid, Susan Baker King Taylor, Pearl Bailey, Josephine Baker, Mary McLeod Bethune, Marita Bonner, Hallie Quinn Brown, Althea Gibson, Sally Hemings, Lena Horne, Nella Larsen, Rosa Parks (one of my personal heroines), Charlotte Ray, Wilma Rudolph, Harriet Tubman, Alice Walker, Ida B. Wells-Barnett, Herman Branson, Ernest E. Just, Samuel Lee Kountz, Jr., Kenneth Olden, Maurice Rabb, George E. Alcorn, Otis Boykin, George Wash. Carver, Frederick M. Jones, Elijah McCoy, John P. Parker, Rufus Stokes, Granville T. Woods, Albert G. Crenshaw, Charles R. Drew, Roscoe L. Koontz, Samuel L. Kountz, William A. Hinton, Lovell A. Jones, Daniel Hale Williams, Archibald Alexander, Clarence Elder, Roscoe C. Giles, Campbell Johnson, Caldwell McCoy, and John B. Slaughter. And the list goes on and on!

ETHNICITY

"It is a great shock at the age of five or six to find that in a
world of Gary Coopers, you are an Indian."
(James Baldwin, Speech, 1965)

"All Latinos are good lovers." "Most Brits are a bit
stuffy." "All French citizen despise American tourists."
"Scots are more than a bit frugal with their money."
"Japanese students test well in mathematics and science."
"White men can't jump!" (Last quote is from a popular
basketball movie with Woody Harrelson). Are these true
statements? Sure, at least for *some* Latinos, Brits, French,
Scots, Japanese, and White basketball players. But these
statements are also false for *some* Latinos, Brits, French,
Scots, Japanese, and White basketball players.

Although America touts itself as a melting pot
where people of different ethnic origins can blend together,
the melting and the blending have not always been easy.
For example, at the end of the nineteenth century and the
beginning of the twentieth century, America needed
immigrants – lots of them. Cheap labor was needed for

building railroads, working in the mills, and digging coal out of the mines. Italians, Poles, Chinese, and other ethnic groups were welcomed to our shores with open arms--as laborers, but not necessarily as neighbors.

Like little enclaves, Polish, Italian, Jewish, and Czech communities, as well as Chinatowns, sprung up in American cities. When immigrants came to our shores, they brought with them not only their strong backs, but also their food, dress, language, and religion. Pity the young Anglo-Saxon girl from the "right side of the tracks" who was caught trying to date the young Italian boy from the "wrong side of the tracks." Pity the hard-working young Polish man who tried to break into a union dominated by non-Poles.

In schools, immigrant children faced numerous problems, not the least of which was having teachers who looked down their noses (e.g., conveyed negative expectations) at these strange-sounding, strange-looking, and, sometimes, strange-smelling youngsters. The lack of parent-teacher interaction, certainly hindered by parents who could not speak English, did not help matters.

Culturally, how are ethnic minority children any different from the mainstream (Anglo), middle-class teachers and administrators who run today's schools? Would knowing the distinctive traits of minority students better prepare educators to enter classrooms? Hispanic children, for instance, may possess several traits that potentially could bring them into conflict with mainstream peers and teachers.

As one example, Hispanic children, especially Chicanos, prefer activities in which they can achieve a goal with other students rather than being in competition with them. This attitude toward competition flies in the face of some mainstream teachers and students who believe in the survival of the fittest and have no qualms about achieving at another's expense.

As another example, ethnic role models (e.g., especially within the professions) for Hispanics are hard to find. It may be harder for Hispanic students (and their teachers) to set high academic and career goals because they believe, realistically, they will never be able to achieve them.

At times, it is almost as if teachers believe a positive halo-effect exists for some students (e.g., Asians) and a negative halo-effect exists for other students (e.g., Blacks, Hispanics). Some students are seen as destined for greatness; others are not. The relationship between students' ethnicity and teachers' occupational expectations for these students has been researched.

In this research, Anglo, Hispanic, Black, and Asian elementary students' future occupational status was predicted by teachers. Among the findings was the fact that Asian students were likely to be classified into higher occupational categories on the prestige continuum than other ethnic groups. On the contrary, Black students were more likely to be assigned to the unskilled labor category.

Other research concludes that teachers do not expect Mexican-American children or other minority children, as a group, to excel in school. Ethnic bias exists and, through the self-fulfilling prophecy, is likely to be conveyed to students. Teachers also do not expect Hispanic parents, perhaps due to language barriers or unfamiliarity with the school system, to get involved in their children's education.

When expectations are low, as they are in schools for many ethnic minorities, one can expect students to "live down" to those expectations. School becomes a hostile place where only failure, and more failure, is expected – first by the teachers and then by the students, themselves. Soon school is seen as a place from which to escape, from which to drop out. Among the factors that principals believe contribute to high Hispanic student dropout levels are low achievement, lack of parental support, truancy, and *low teacher expectations*. Might it be that low teacher expectations "cause" some of the other factors?

One's ethnicity often is revealed in one's language. In schools, bilingual education is usually provided to non-mainstream Americans. Research, using teachers of first- and second-grade students, revealed that these teachers had lower expectations of students with lower English proficiency.

Even before teachers have formally met their minority students, they may have formed negative expectations of them. How is this possible? Students' records, complete with enough information to identify students' ethnicity, among other things, normally would be available to teachers before the start of the school year.

Then again, being a minority student might be an advantage. For instance, many educators hold only positive expectations for Japanese-American students, believing that they are well-behaved, smart, quiet, and that they get good grades.

Are teachers somewhat surprised when one of their Chinese, Korean, or Japanese students does not do well, but less surprised when one of their Jones, Brown, or Smith students (from a nearby minority housing project) does poorly? Probably.

If teachers have a stake in having their preconceived notions (e.g., their expectations) come true, then, at least for Japanese-American (as well as other Asian) students, the future looks bright. For most other ethnic minority students, the future may not be so encouraging.

The future for some ethnic minorities may well look bleak because the predictions are that we will, for the foreseeable future, continue to have White middle-class educators, complete with their expectations, teaching ever more diverse student bodies.

What can you do to help your child?
- *Read, read, read* stories to your child about heroes and heroines who reflect your child's ethnicity. Many of these people may not regularly appear in a school's curriculum.

- See if your child's school has a plan or policy of adding curriculum materials that are more ethnically diverse.

- Volunteer to serve on school committees that have some say-so in selecting library books, reading materials, etc., to help insure that the offerings are balanced when it comes to ethnicity.

- Arrange for your child to meet successful people of your child's ethnicity who work in a variety of careers –

especially those representing careers with which the child might not regularly come in contact. Most folks are flattered when asked to share their life-long career passion with a child.

- Allow your children to watch appropriate television programs in which persons of their ethnicity are positively portrayed and no ethnic stereotype is evident.

- Discuss with your child examples and stories that reflect proud moments from one's ethnic background, in general, and from one's family, in particular. When your child enters school, he or she may well have opportunities to share--with pride--some of these stories with his or her classmates.

Add your own ideas!

- _____
- _____
- _____
- _____
- _____
- _____

HISPANIC HEROES / HEROINES

Among your author's personal favorites are Walt Disney (I live just a few miles away from Disney World), Pablo Picasso, César Romero, and Lauro Cavazos (once held the position of Secretary of Education for the United States).

Others include, Pedro Antonio de Alarcón, Vasco Núñez de Balbao, Vicente Blasco Ibanez,Simón Bolívar, Pedro Vázquez de Coronado, Hernán Cortés, Celia Cruz, Xavier Cugat, Salvador Dali, Rubén Darío, Juan de la Cierva, Luis de León, Hernando De Soto, Gerardo Diego, Plácido Domingo, José Echegaray Manuel de Falla, David Farragut, Carlos Finlay, Carlos Fuentes, Federico García Lorca, Baltasar Gracián, Enrique Granados, Juan Gris, Rita Hayworth, Bernardo Houssay, Dolores Ibarruri, Pedro Infante, José Ingenieros, Benito Juárez, Ruy López, Mario Molina, Ricardo Montalbán, Rita Moreno, Queen Isabella of Castille, Diegor Rivera, Francisco de Zorrilla, Angela Salinas and Lee Treviño.   And the list goes on and on!

SOCIO-ECONOMIC STATUS

"The quality of our expectations determines the quality of
our action."
(Andre Gordin, *Thought*, December 1950)

When you are at the grocery store checkout counter
waiting in line and observe someone in front of you
"paying" for his or her order with government-supplied
food stamps and you are paying with cold, hard-earned
cash, what thoughts go through your mind? Do you have a
tendency to size up this person negatively and wonder why
the individual doesn't get a job and pay his or her own way
just like everyone else – just like you? Or, do you give the
person the benefit of the doubt and simply thank God (or
someone) that you don't need such government help?

Perhaps your judgments, in other words, your
expectations, are influenced by an investigative report of
food stamp fraud and abuse that was on the television the
night before. No matter what influenced your expectations,
different people will have different expectations and, as
predicted by the self-fulfilling prophecy, will exhibit
differential behaviors.

Americans are becoming more and more polarized. It can be argued that this polarization can be attributed much more to the fact that we have created an ever-widening socioeconomic or social status gulf between the haves and the have-nots, than to any differences in our skin color or ethnicity. The have-nots are envious and distrustful of the haves, while the haves are threatened by and show disdain for the have-nots.

In schools, the haves and the have-nots are easily identified. Cumulative record files and other student records reveal which students live on which "side of the tracks," which students qualify for free or reduced-price breakfast and lunch programs, and which students come from single-parent, sometimes no parent, homes – sometimes no homes at all! The students, themselves, advertise their socioeconomic status in the clothes they wear, the jewelry they adorn themselves with, and the sheen to their hair. Even in schools where the students wear uniforms, the haves and the have-nots are known by everyone, including teachers.

My wife and I made a conscious effort to take advantage of the fact that teachers are predisposed to expect more of students coming from a relatively higher socioeconomic strata and/or educational level. For the first day of school, we made sure that David and Rebecca were "bright-eyed and bushy-tailed." Their hair was recently cut or trimmed, they had new (not necessarily expensive) school clothes and school supplies (e.g., book bag, notebooks, pens), they were well scrubbed, their fingernails were clean, and their teeth were brushed.

We made it a point to attend each and every scheduled "Parents Night" for David and Rebecca and, without sounding too high and mighty, let it be known that I had a Ph.D. and taught at a major university and that my wife had an M. A. and was the head of the English Department at a local high school. It also was known that David and Rebecca accompanied my wife and me on sabbatical for a year in England and 7-months in Australia. All of this added up to, at least in the minds of David's and Rebecca's teachers, our having an above-average social status – even though I drove a 20-year old car and my wife drove a Saturn with over 130,000 miles on it.

Social status in a community can be viewed a number of ways. Sometimes family structure (whether one is from a divorced or an intact family) conveys social status. As evidence of this, one study had female undergraduate college students majoring in preschool teacher education view videotapes of a preschool boy and girl and then rate the children. One group was told that the boy and girl in the tapes were from a divorced family – often accompanied by a lowered family income, and the other group was told that the children were from an intact family. The reviewers rated divorced-home children significantly lower than intact children on personality traits and predicted school behaviors.

The implications for children entering school are clear. Students' family status can trigger expectations for which, according to self-fulfilling prophecy theory, teachers are only too willing to seek verifying evidence.

Sometimes teachers' expectations of students are formed not by who the students are as individuals but, instead, by the mere fact that the students are seen to be part of a larger group. The expectations, then, that are held for the larger group, extend to individual students. Who you "rub elbows" with can make all the difference in the world in the expectations others hold for you. Recall the "Your daughter has fallen in with the wrong crowd!" story presented earlier in this book.

Another study asked suburban primary school teachers to predict the academic success of their students through the rest of the year, through high school, and through college. The teachers were divided into groups – those who taught high SES (socioeconomic status) students and those who taught average or low SES. It was found that teachers in high SES classrooms had higher expectations for student academic achievement than did their counterparts in average or low SES schools.

Do students of differing socioeconomic levels pick up on teachers' differential expectations and the differential behaviors that follow? Yes! Lower income students often feel that teachers dislike them personally and favor students from higher-income families. Higher-income or higher-social status students, on the other hand, take it for granted that teachers like them.

Social status, as an expectation-forming factor, often can be correlated with other factors such as race and ethnicity – that is, many minorities are also economically disadvantaged and/or rank lower on social status measures. Given that teachers often are of a different social class, race, and/or ethnicity than that of their students, it is doubly important that teachers are aware of the preconceived stereotypes that they may bring into their classrooms.

How much of teachers' attitudes toward students is based upon their knowledge of which "side of the tracks" students come from – Pill Hill, where all the doctors live, or Harrison Village, the primarily Black housing project near the river? Do students' clothes and their condition – that is, whether they are clean, recently pressed, in style (all signs of higher or lower socioeconomic status) – influence how teachers act toward students?

When counseling students regarding their future career choices, do teachers tend to see some students as more likely to be successful in a vocational-technical career (just like the student's parents), while seeing other students as more likely to be successful in a professional or managerial career (just like the student's parents)? Is there any correlation between what teachers see as reasonable career paths for students and what teachers know about the students' socioeconomic level?

Higher socioeconomic status often gets students greater teacher and peer attention. For instance, whether it is asking elementary school students to recall what they did over the summer or asking high school students how they plan to spend their upcoming Christmas vacation, chances are that higher socioeconomic-level children will have more interesting and exciting responses – they traveled to Key West in Florida, went to Williamsburg, Virginia, or will be going to Vale, Colorado, to ski or to St. Johns in the British Virgin Islands to sail. In comparison, what can the lower socioeconomic-level child, who plans to spend the summer playing in the city streets, have to say that will be as interesting?

As a personal example, my wife and two children (David and Rebecca) joined me for my year's sabbatical at Durham University in northern England and, later, for a 7-month sabbatical at the University of Melbourne in Australia. My social status as college professor, where sabbatical opportunities are available, gave our children a rare opportunity that most lower socioeconomic-status children do not enjoy. Each time our children returned home and started back to school, their experiences made them the center of attention in the eyes of both teachers and fellow students.

What can you do to help your child?

- When moving, if possible, select a recognized high-achieving school district. Indicators of such schools can include, but are not limited to, those where high standardized test scores are earned (e.g., SATs), a high percentage of students go on to some form of post-secondary education, and where a number of honors-type courses are offered. The positive expectations for students that teachers (as well as peers) in these school's hold should rub off on the student – including your child(ren).

- Although some parents' choices may be limited by finances, sometimes homes in such good school districts are as reasonable as anywhere else--it just takes a little investigative work by parents to find out which schools are the "good" schools. Take time to meet with the principal of the school where your child would be attending if you moved into that school district. Ask about the school's curriculum, test scores, discipline policy, special programs, and any other items of interest to you.

- When visiting a school, observe the students during that school day as you tour the facility. You should come away with a real "feel," one way or the other about that school. Further benefits of, in effect, "interviewing" perspective principals and taking a tour of the school, are the positive expectations formed in the minds of your hosts. The image is, "Here are parents who really care about their child's education."

- Consider selecting a school, public or private, where uniforms are required because uniforms may negate some of the social differences among children.

- Contact your local school district for information regarding their possible School Choice options where parents can choose, within guidelines, what school within the district their child will attend. Parents who are knowledgeable of School Choice options are in a position to exercise those options. Parents who remain ignorant of these options, end up taking whatever schools that are "left over." Normally, these are not the higher quality schools.

- Pursue the availability of government vouchers as a way to offset the costs of sending a child to a school other than the one in one's immediate neighborhood. At the same time, don't overlook a great school locally. A few miles from me is a small elementary school in a small economically depressed fishing village. Looks can be deceiving. The fact is that the school has been judged as an "A" school by the state for the last three years in a row! Any parent would be happy to have a child enrolled in this school.

- Stay aware of the ratings your child's school earns (e.g., as a result of FCATs in Florida) each year. Poor rating for several years may entitle you to send your child to a better performing school – with government support.

Add your own ideas!

- _____
- _____
- _____
- _____
- _____
- _____

WORD GAP

"Vocabulary unexpectedly emerged as a justification for discrimination in classrooms serving mostly children of Latinx immigrants."
(Adair, *et al.*)

The word gap among students is so important to teachers forming first impressions that it simply had to be singled out! From as early as possible in your child's life help him or her to develop a wide vocabulary. Research shows that there is a "Word Gap" among children when they arrive at school. Teachers immediately notice this gap. A child's vocabulary (or lack thereof) is one of the first things teachers use to "peg," "size up" or form student "expectations."

B. Hart & T. R. Risley, (*American Educator*, Spring 2003) report that "In four years, the average child in a professional family would accumulate experience with almost 45 million words, an average child in a working-class family 26 million words, and an average child in a welfare family of 13 million words. This disparity in

hearing words from parents and caregivers translates directly into a disparity in **learning** words" – the basis of most formal schooling. This disparity is staggering; it is shocking! It *may* be possible to catch up, but it would be so much easier if a child were to arrive at the school door steps already possessing a solid vocabulary. The authors describe this as an "early catastrophe" that can have lasting detrimental effects on the academic achievement of lower income children.

The concept behind Hart and Risley's findings is supported by Adair, *et al.*, in their 2017 article titled, "How the word gap argument negatively impacts young children of Latinx immigrants' conceptualizations of learning," published in the *Harvard Educational Review*, 67(3)309-334.

But, like most research, there may be another side. First, we hear eggs are bad for you and then we hear they are good for you. A glass of red wine is fine, or is it? Who to believe? What to believe? More recent studies of the word gap suggest that the gap between high-income and low-income groups is about 4 million, not 30 million. Should this make low-income parents feel comforted?

Here is where parents, grandparents, and caregivers can help. In some homes, children lack opportunities to engage in meaningful conversation with parents and/or significant caregivers. Sitting around the dinner table, discussing the day's local events, sometime even world events, sometimes upcoming events, occurs often in some families yet is absent in others. Read, read, read to your child. Have your child read, read, read to you. All of these conversations and interactions help build a child's vocabulary.

These children get to have verbal exchanges that not only allow them to hear, and thus learn, new vocabulary, but also provides them with a chance to interact with adults as "equals," in a give-and-take way where the child gets to practice using his or her vocabulary as a tool to influence others at the dinner table. This experience will serve him well in school, and later, in life situations.

For other children the only vocabulary building opportunities that occur often fall into short, one way, child/adult exchanges such as "shut up," "sit down," "go outside and play," "be quiet" or, even worse, being ignored completely.

The three most important words in real estate are *location, location, location*. The three most important words in education may well be *vocabulary, vocabulary, vocabulary*, because vocabulary so heavily influences a teacher's *expectations, expectations, expectations*! One impacts the other!

Keep in mind that as you look for ways to cast your child in the best light in a teacher's eyes (e.g., her expectations), you can only do what you can do. Many expectations-triggering factors (race, gender, ethnicity, height) cannot reasonably be altered, but vocabulary development can be – start now, start often to help build your child's vocabulary. He or she will thank you for it. I know that his or her teachers will thank you.

OTHER EXPECTATION-TRIGGERING FACTORS

"Men have a trick of coming up to what is expected of them, good or bad."
(J. Riis, The Author's Kalendar, 1911)

There are, of course, many other human factors that are capable of triggering expectations in the minds of others – including teachers. Several of these factors will be discussed briefly. Still other factors simply will be listed, and it will be left to the reader's imagination to predict the expectations such factors can trigger.

Below are a number of additional factors than can, and do, trigger expectations from others. The fact is that there is *NOTHING* about human beings that is incapable capable of triggering expectations – choice of toe nail color, wearing sandals or sneakers, having a delicate or an outrageous tattoo, wearing a one piece or two piece swimming suit, eating with your elbows on the table, putting salt on food even before tasting it, etc. Because the list of triggering factors would be too long, they simply could not all be listed here. In fact, it would be much easier to list all the human factors that are NOT capable of triggering expectations. That list would be very short – it would be zero!

Feel free to add your own expectation-triggering factors to this list.

- **Birth Order – First, Middle, Last**

What does the research have to say about "first born" children? "last born" children? "middle-born" children? It is clear that more is expected of first-born children. They are expected to be outgoing, obedient, responsible, achievers, and leaders. Last-born children are expected to be likable, sociable, and popular followers, on the one hand, but low on obedience and achievement on the other hand. Middle children are best described as balanced. They are good mediators and have superior cooperation skills because they, unlike, first-borns, never have parents all to themselves. Therefore, they must negotiate for their fair share. Last born children (youngest) are typically outgoing, lower academic achievers, often rebellious, and tend to be most liberal.

- **Only Child**

Only children are expected to be academically oriented and higher achievers, but usually more self-centered and not particularly likable. At least until siblings come along, they have their parents, and their parents' resources, all to themselves. These children are often perfectionists, conservative, and leaders. They may be expected to have adjustment difficulties when attending preschool or kindergarten where they must share the attention of the adult in power, the teacher, with twenty or thirty other children. Note, of the first twenty-three astronauts sent into outer space by the U.S., twenty-one were only-children or first-borns. Could this be just a coincidence?

- **Knowledge of Siblings**

If it is true that you are judged by the company that you keep, it certainly follows that you are judged by siblings who have preceded you. When teachers are overheard saying, "Oh, oh, here comes another one of the kids from the Smith or Jones family," the message is loud and clear. This latest Smith or Jones kid is expected to be much like his or her older brother or sister. After all, apples do not fall far from the tree, do they?

I am sure that many readers have found themselves in the situation of having to follow a particularly good or particularly bad brother or sister (e.g., achievement and/or behavior) through the grades in school. For some, this was a real benefit. For others who had older siblings with "tarnished" or "exceptional" scholastic and/or behavior records, the path through school was more difficult.

- **Single or Two Parent Homes**

Do teachers expect different things from different children depending upon whether they come from a single parent or two-parent family? If the single-parent is female (and most single parents are), do teachers worry, especially for boys, that discipline might be lax at home? Do teachers worry that children from these families will have less attention devoted to them? For instance, will a single parent, tired from a hard day of work and from having to do all the chores usually shared between two parents, have the time and energy to monitor a child's homework, read to him or her, or help with a required school project? Perhaps yes; perhaps no!

- **Latch-Key Children**

    When teachers know that children are returning home after school to empty, unsupervised homes, where the kids literally use their own key to unlock the latch to the front door, do they (the teachers) form expectations of the children? Of the parents? Might these expectations be influenced by how a particular teacher feels about the lack of after-school parental supervision?

- **Working Parent(s)**

    On the one hand, might teachers' expectations be positively influenced by knowing that both of a child's parents are industrious enough to hold down a full-time job? On the other hand, might these same teachers' expectations be negatively influenced by the knowledge that neither parent is accessible to contact or to visit with during the day if a problem should arise? Might some teachers think that when both parents work that they might just have their priorities all mixed up? Might the answers to these questions vary from teacher to teacher?

- **Height of Child**

    Short people and tall people often are vertically challenged, as well as discriminated against. Woe be the teenage boy who is extra short for his age or the middle school girl who towers over her male classmates. Studies show that short people are discriminated against in the work world. According to a *St. Petersburg Times* article (October 18, 2003), researchers found that "each extra inch of height equals $789 a year, which is bad news for short people." One's love life, too, can be impacted by height. Studies have shown that women generally are reluctant to even date very short men, thus precluding the opportunity for a more involved or lasting intimate relationship.

- **A.M. or P.M. Kindergarten Children**

Providing that a school district provides parents with a choice, which children, a.m. kindergarten or p.m. kindergarten, might teachers expect more from? Often teachers expect more from a.m. kindergarten children, perhaps because they believe that parents who get up early in the morning to get their child off to school are, themselves, working, industrious, and interested in "getting a jump" on life. The belief is that these positive parental attitudes will be instilled in their children, thus making the teacher's job easier.

Children who attend p.m. kindergartens may be perceived as coming from homes where parents don't have to get up early in the morning to go to work and, instead, sleep in until most of morning is frittered away. This lack of a work ethic might rub off on the parents' children, too.

- **Color of Hair**

What do we know about (e.g., expect from) blondes? Just think of all the jokes that have been made at the expense of blondes. What do we expect from someone who has fiery red hair? Is being told that one has "mousy brown" hair a compliment or a put-down? In either case it is an evaluation, an expectation, of sorts. In Iceland, people with light brown hair earn more money than blonds.

- **How Hair is Worn**

What do people expect from a boy who has a "butch" haircut? A boy who wears his hair half-way down his back? A boy who shaves off all of his hair? A boy who wears his hair "like a girl"? What do people expect from a girl who wears her hair much longer or much shorter than the norm for the school? A girl who wears her hair up all the time? A girl who "streaks" or otherwise colors her hair? A girl who wears her hair "like a boy"?

- **Biting Fingernails**

Some kids do; some kids don't. What does it imply if a child does bite his or her nails? Does it mean he or she is naturally nervous and, thus, should not be put under any extra-special demands, made class president, selected to give a speech, asked to demonstrate a science technique. What do you suppose teachers think (e.g., expect)?

- **Condition of Clothes**

What do middle-class teachers think (e.g., expect) of students who come to school with dirty, wrinkled, and sometimes urine-smelling clothes? Do they think that the student's parents must not care much about the child's welfare and, if this is the case, probably do not care much about the child's schooling? After all, how much effort does it take to send children off to school with washed and ironed clothes? In some families it takes both time and money that is not readily available.

- **Quality of Clothes**

Where uniforms are not required it is quite easy for the trained eye to notice who is wearing trendy or name brand (often more costly). This may suggest to the teacher that this child is from a family of means that could spill over into where the child lives, whether the child takes vacations, etc. Where uniforms are required it is still possible for the trained eye to spot newer, well pressed outfits, perhaps with more expensive adornments.

- **Where a Child Chooses to Sit**

I jokingly tell my college students on the first day of class, while pointing to the first row, second row, and so on, of seats, "This is the A row, the B row, the C row and – well, you get the picture don't you?" When given a choice, better students sit closer to the teacher, while other students – especially those prone to misbehave – sit farthest away from the teacher. This voluntary seat selection does not go unnoticed by teachers who may use this information to help them form their first impressions. Students would be well advised to choose their classroom seats carefully.

- **Personal Hygiene**

Because I was tall as a child, I often was seated towards the back of the classroom. I remember once in either second or third grade that I was seated next to a girl whose name was Nellie Barnes. As I recall, Ms. Barnes was not especially tall. The reason that she was seated in the back of the room was because she smelled – she smelled just like the inside of a barn. Really, this is a true story. I suppose that the teacher could not stand the smell either, so she had placed Ms. Barnes as far away from her as possible.

What do teachers expect from children, and from children's parents, when children are sent to school without any obvious concern for even basic personal hygiene? Body odors are strong. Fingernails are dirty. Hands and other body parts that can be seen appear not to have been washed for some time. Teeth are discolored and obviously not brushed. It should come as no surprise that teachers form negative expectations of both the children and the children's parents. Sometimes it reaches the level of repulsion!

STILL MORE EXPECTATION-TRIGGERING FACTORS

"Our circumstances answer to our expectations and the demand of our natures."
(Henry David Thoreau)

Here are still some more factors that can trigger expectations in the minds of teachers! You can fill in the expectations – positive or negative – that are likely to be generated in the minds of your child's teachers as these factors are exhibited by you or your child. Many of these factors are relied upon by teachers, especially in preschool, kindergarten or early elementary grades where other "evidence" is missing, to form initial impressions or expectations.

- Child's Manners or Lack There Of
  Even a simple "thank you" is a good sign.

- Child's Eye Contact with a Teacher

Is eye-contact returned or avoided?

- Firmness of Child's Handshake
  Is it wimpy or does it convey confidence?

- Color of Child's Eyes
  Whether or not we like it, often the "eyes" have it.
  Think Paul Neuman.

- Child's Ability to Spell his or her Name
  Cleary this ability should have been mastered.

- Child's Knowledge of his or her Address
  For safety, at least, this is important.

- Child's Excessive Use of Makeup
  There is no real norm other than the one the teacher
  or school holds.

- Child's Ability to Follow Directions
  This should have been practiced well before coming
  to school.

- Child's Sneakers Untied with Long, Floppy, Laces
  Dragging on the Floor
  Besides being dangerous, it may send the wrong
  message.

- Child Chews Gum
  Pretty obvious, one should not be doing this in
  school.

- Child Chews Snuff

Sure it does happen, but it would not be welcomed by teachers.

- Child is Adopted
  Doesn't mean a thing – or does it?

- Child's Parents Provide Snacks when Requested
  Where parents, on behalf of a child, can help that is a good sign.

- Child's Parents Accompany him or her to School the First Day (perhaps, even to the classroom door, itself!)
  There is such a thing as over-stepping the boundaries.

- Parents Sign and Return Notes, Forms, and Homework Sent Home
  Teacher parent communication is important.

- One or Both of the Child's Parents Come for Parents' Nights
  Those attending will be remembered.

Literally, 1000s more human characteristics could follow that are capable of triggering teacher expectations including, the color of a child's fingernail polish to an obviously unattended to bad tooth, to having socks that do not match.

PRAISE: ITS IMPACT UPON EXPECTATIONS

"He was swimming in a sea of other's expectations. Men have drowned in seas like that." (Robert Jordan)

Expectations, positive or negative, are going to be delivered "come hell or high water." Although body language can speak volumes, sometimes even more than the spoken language, the fact is that we heavily rely upon verbal messages to convey and to receive expectations. We use verbal languatge (accompanied by gestures) to send our expectations, and we decipher the verbal expectation messages that are delivered to us. In either case, when we send our verbal expectations or we receive the expectations of others, we get the message. And, when bombarded with these messages over and over again for long periods of time, we *really* get the message.

Praise too often is taken as a good thing when, in fact, there are numerous situations where the deliverer of praise should be cautious. For instance, praise often is seen as an evaluation - it is intended to manipulate, shape or control a receiver. The sender of the praise expects us to comply! Even if the sender did not intend praise to do this, it doesn't matter. It only mattters how the person interprets the received praise. If he or she sees it as an evaluation, which most often it is, then that is exactly what it is!

Among still other cautions centering around delivering praise is that it can be seen as an attempt to flatter, it causes unwanted physiological reactions (e.g., blushing, increased heartbeat), it often ends in a "but," it often benefits the sender more than the receiver, it can become addictive, it may contribute to narcisim, and it often stifles risk-taking.

The bottom line is that praising is capable of conveying positive expectations. But, because praise is is an evaluation, the receiver realizes that the lack of praise, especially expected praise, can convey negative expectations. Praise is like a coin, it has two sides.

If these cautions are true, and they are, then those wishing to convey expectations might just have to look elsewhere for how to do it. For a detailed discussion of the cautions surrounding the use of praise, please see the book, *PRAISE LESS ENCOURAGE MORE: Judge, Evaluate and Manipulate Less; Fortify, Galvanize, Embolden and Influence More*, by your author, Robert T. Tauber.

After identifying the cautions about delivering praise, the book goes on to offer a preferred alternative – encouragement. Praise and encouragement are **NOT** synonyms. Just like apples are apples, and oranges are oranges, praise is praise, and encouragement is encouragement. After reading this book, most readers commit to stopping or seriously curtailing the use of praise.

MRS. SMITH TEACHING TO HER STUDENTS' IQ!

"I'm not in this world to live up to your expectations and you're are not in this world to live up to mine."
(Bruce Lee)

It was early in the school year and Mrs. Smith (not her real name), a 2nd grade teacher in a western Pennsylvania school district, realized that she was short some supplies for her class – several tablets and pencils. She went to the principal's office and was just about to ask for her supplies when the principal's secretary burst in to say that there was a problem in the outer office. The principal went out to see what was up. Mrs. Smith, standing next to the principal's desk, did what all curious people would do – she looked! What did she see? She saw her 2nd grade class roster complete with the students' IQs (measure of intelligence). She quickly jotted down the IQs.

The principal came back in, Mrs. Smith got her needed supplies, and the school year started.

Mrs. Smith used her new-found knowledge about her students in several ways. She grouped the students by IQ – redbirds, bluebirds, jaybirds. She called on students, taking into consideration their IQ – easier questions for students with lower IQs and more challenging questions for students with higher IQs. She also gave students with higher IQs more time to compose their answers to questions. So as not to embarrass or humiliate students whith lower IQs, the teacher would quickly move on to another student to answer. Assignments, too, were handed out using IQs as a determining factor. Finally, she handed out classroom responsibilities – hall monitor, taking attendance slips to the office, etc., to students with the higher IQ. Lower IQ students dusted erasers, cleaned the chalk trays, and did other mundane chores.

When Mrs. Smith calculated her final grades, she was not the least bit surprised. Students with higher IQs earned significantly higher grades than did students with lower IQs. The correlation between IQs and grades was almost perfect.

Afterall, what would you expect? Surely, those with the higher level of intelligence would do better than those with less intelligence (e.g., IQ). In turn, they would earn higher grades. This cannot be a surprise to anyone.

A sample of the results are shown below.
Name.............IQ........Final Grade
Karen M...........99.............."C"
Susan R.........141.............."A+"

Elmer T.........101..............."C"
Larry M...........91..............."D"
Sharon C........106..............."C+"
Randy K.........122..............."B"
Jarvis K...........92..............."D"
Melanie D.......131..............."A-"

.

The school year ended and Mrs. Smith attended the final teachers' meeting with the principal. The principal congratulated the teachers on the fine job they had done during the year and asked, "Does anyone have any suggestions for how we could do an even better job teaching next year?" Mrs. Smith raised her hand. She said that she thought it would be a good idea for all teachers to be given their students' IQs and supported her suggestion by relating the details of how she had used her students' IQs in her teaching.

When Mrs. Smith ended her story the principal asked, "How did you get the students' IQs"? Mrs. Smith's face turned a bit red as she told how she had copied them off the principal's desk at the start of the year. The principal's mouth fell open and he was almost in shock. He announced, "Mrs. Smith, those were not the students' IQs, they were the students' locker numbers!" **Mrs. Smith had been teaching all year long to the students' locker numbers.** Sure enough, students had lived up to (or down to) these locker numbers. Let's just hope that if your child had been in this class that he or she had been assigned a high locker number.

On a personal note, each time I check my mail, deposited in a common area along with all other residents in my community, I regularly note that my low numbered box is towards the bottom, just a foot above the ground. I'm sure that its placement down there does not mean anything. At least I don't think that it means anything. To play it safe, though, I may petition for a box to be moved towards the top of the stack! Maybe I will claim that I have back problems and cannot easily bend over.

Thanks to Mike Wison for his locker-student classroom sketch.

HOW SOME TEACHERS DIFFERENTIALLY TREAT HIGH- AND LOW-EXPECTATIONS STUDENTS

" As a man gets wiser, he expects less, and probably gets
more than he expects."
(Joseph Farrell, *Lectures of a Certain Professor*)

By this point in the book, hopefully it has been made clear that various and sundry human characteristics do trigger expectations in the minds of others – including teachers. Simply put, teachers are human beings, first, and teachers, second. Hence, they are not immune to the self-fulfilling prophecy when it comes to the treatment of their students.

Just how some teachers differentially treat high- and low-expectations students already has been discussed, whether it be with respect to disciplining misconduct, grading student essays, or predicting career paths for children.

Specifically, though, there are a number of very observable and well researched in-class behaviors that teachers engage in that can convey their high or low expectations of children. Although some of these have been addressed earlier, they deserve further discussion.

Among the ways that teachers' in-class behaviors differ include:

- Praising low-expectations students more frequently and more excessively than high-expectations students for marginal or inadequate responses. Everyone in the class knows that "dusting erasers" is normally not something we all write home about. The message clearly announces to everyone within earshot who has fallen behind and needs this extra support (e.g., prodding).

- Seating low-expectations students farthest from the teacher and/or seating them all together in a group. The message is, "Students quickly learn what expectations the teachers holds for the student groups labeled 'Blue birds,' 'Red birds,' and 'Black birds.' One teacher grouped her students with the labels, "Indians," "Chiefs," and "Clowns." Throughout the year students seemed to live up to or down to their respective label.

- Waiting less time for low-expectations students to answer before calling on another student to help. The message is, "Yes, I will call on you, but I really don't expect that you will know the answer."

- Providing more wait-time, as well as offering clues or hints to high-expectations students. The message is, "I know that you know the answer, and, in fact, I will give you hints to help you answer correctly." You have a stake in the student's response. If he or she answers correctly, then you have validated your expectation powers!

- Providing more, and more detailed, written comments on the papers of high-expectations students than on the papers of low-expectations students. The message is, "Why waste the time and energy to write comments on low-expectations students' papers? After all, they probably will not read them anyhow!"

- Calling upon low-expectations students to answer less difficult, simple recall questions, while at the same time calling on high-expectations students to answer more difficult questions requiring analytic, interpretative, and evaluative skills. The message is, "Some students are capable, and some students are not capable of handling challenging questions."

- Providing a "look" to low-expectations students that says it all – "I expect very little from you. Don't disappoint me," while, at the same time, providing a look to high-expectations students that says, "I expect a lot from you." Children are uncanny in their ability to read body language, even subtle body language. It is not that hard to do. Even Fido your family pet can easily read your mood the second you get home – he bounds toward you or slinks away.

- Teachers vary their nodding, proximity, eye contact, smiles, and even the "sparkle in their eyes" depending upon whether they expect a lot or a little from students. They also vary their "arrival on time to class," "their class preparation," and their "enthusiasm in teaching" depending upon their audience. These differential behaviors do not go unnoticed by students.

- Criticizing low-expectations students more frequently than high-expectations students for inappropriate classroom behaviors. The message is, "High expectation students really do know better and thus just a simple correction is sufficient for them. On the other hand, low-expectations students are a bit dense and need to be more heavily disciplined."

- Allowing low-expectations students to use the attributes of Luck, Task Difficulty and Ability as reasons (excuses?) for poor performance but helping high-expectations students to see that Effort can often outweigh Luck, Task Difficulty and Ability. Effort, of course, is that one and only one attribute of human nature that can be turned up or turned down by the child, himself or herself. Luck, Task Difficulty and Ability are attributes that cannot directly be changed by the child. Here are several of the more common "Ability" messages parents send their children: "You are so clever," "You are so smart," "You are a real wizz!" and "You are so intelligent." Gee, they flow so easily off our lips, don't they?

- Putting children into tracks or ability-based (usually based, at best, on tests that are only one measure of ability) groups for extended periods with little or no way to change tracks if performance improves. Such groupings place a ceiling (like the glass ceiling for women and other minorities in the workplace) on learning for students in the lower group because they are not exposed to challenging teaching or curricula.

- Jumping to conclusions regarding a student's behavior and achievement whereby, for instance, who one hangs around with is used to influence teachers' judgments and expectations. Recall the story early in this book titled, "You Daughter Has Fallen in With the Wrong Crowd!" Our daughter, Becky, received her first "C" ever, in ten years of schooling, from an Australian history teacher who believed that if Becky was associating with "known non-studiers," then she, too, must be a "non-studier."

- Offering sympathy for low-expectations students, rather than demanding (within reason, of course) that, in spite of personal hardships, school work must be done and done well. Such sympathy can provide some students with a readymade excuse for unacceptable behavior and continued poor achievement. If teachers believe that factors such as "living in a run-down housing project," "having no male authority figure at home," or "being a person of color" excuses children from performing well, then the children, too, will begin to believe (e.g., expect) it. I have heard teachers announce in teacher's rooms, something to the effect, "Well, what can you expect from Joe? He has lived eight different places this year, comes for the other side of the tracks, and has an absent father who is in jail."

- Forming expectations on students' socio-economic, racial or ethnic status. A case in point. When Hispanic students in Jamie Escalante class (featured in the film, *Stand and Deliver*), excelled in a standardized mathematics class, they were forced to repeat the exam because the examiners simply could not believe that these kids could possibly have scored as high as they did. Imagine how these students felt when their hard-earned test results were questioned!

Please keep in mind that these differential (high-expectations and low-expectations) teacher behaviors are not a one time occurrence. Once started they are likely to continue day after day, month after month, and year after year. For the high-expectations' students this is great! For the low-expectations' students, not so much.

Personal confession

The Jamie Escalante example, above, caused me to think about how I have treated students who excelled when I had not expected them to do so (e.g., they did better on a test, project, or paper than predicted). I can recall rescoring such student's work because I just knew I must have made a mistake in grading. He or she simply could not have done that well. I can recall closing my eyes and "picturing" who was sitting near the student in question, and then reexamining their work, too, to see if it was the same as the student's in question. Perhaps the student cheated off his classmates and that would explain his or her better-than-expected performance. Almost reluctantly, I had to admit, on more than one occasion, that I simply had misjudged the student's capabilities!

A classic study on teacher expectations

A classic study of teacher expectations was done by Rist (1970) and reported in an article titled, "Student social class and teacher expectations: The self-fulfilling prophecy in ghetto education." It was published in *Harvard Educational Review*, 40(411-451). Rist observed the criteria an urban kindergarten teacher appeared to use in order to seat her students at three tables (Tables 1, 2, & 3), and then recorded her interactions with these students throughout the school year. Once table placement was assigned, a sort of caste system developed.

Students placed at Table 1, the table closest to the teacher, were most like the teacher, herself - well dressed, spoke standard American English, and were from families with higher levels of education where both parents worked. Table 1 students were her "ideal" students, they were high-expectations students. By contrast, students placed at Table 3, the table furthest away from the teacher, were most often poorly dressed, carried a smell of urine, had matted or unprocessed hair, were from families on welfare, and responded to the teacher using a Black dialect. These low-expectations students did not look, smell, act, or talk like the teacher.

As the year progressed, less and less attention was paid to the Table 3 students, except to discipline them. By the end of the year, Table 1 students had excelled, Table 3 students had not. The first grade and, later, second grade, teachers continued the kindergarten teacher's original groupings **even though the groupings were not based upon any legitimate factors relating to ability or achievement**. No surprise, then, to learn that Table 1 students (high-expectations students) excelled and Table 3 students (low-expectations students) did poorly in 1st and 2nd grade. The students' academic success was determined on the first day of school!

For some students, once low expectations regarding their success had been planted in a mind of teachers, they now had twelve years to look forward to receiving these low expectations-type messages. Many of these kids will take the only way out – quit school and, at least temporarily, escape the low expectations messages bombardment from teachers. The problem is that they simply escape from the pot into the fire. Still more low expectation messages await them, those who drop out of school.

WHAT ELSE CAN YOU DO TO INFLUENCE THE EXPECTATIONS OF YOUR CHILD'S TEACHER?

"If you accept the expectations of others, especially
negative ones,
then you never will change the outcome."
(Michael Jordan)

Keep in mind that the following suggestions are presented in no special order of importance. Address them as you are able/willing to do so. Don't go overboard on any of them.

1. Consider getting your child's hair cut or trimmed. Make this one of several pre-school events that you and your child take part in.

2. Consider "taking your child to lunch" as a way of celebrating the beginning of the school year. Use

this time to discuss any concerns your child might be facing.

3. Take your young child for a "walk-through" around the school building and, if possible, through the school pointing out his or her room, entrances and exits, office, toilets, cafeteria, etc.

4. As, ahead of time, for a copy of the school's rules and procedures that students are to follow. Go over pertinent portions of these materials with your child before school starts.

5. If uniforms or other school materials are required, get them well before school is scheduled to begin. Consider looking for "recycled" uniforms sold by parents' groups.

6. Avoid "trending" or what may only be acceptable as on-the-street clothes (e.g., sagging pants, very short skirts, under garments showing) if they are likely to be a classroom distraction.

7. Send your children to school every day – except, of course, if they are too ill to attend! Students cannot learn if they are not in school. "Getting the notes" from a fellow student and/or "making up" missed school work simply is not the same as being there when the material was taught.

8. Send you child to school on time! Promptness is a recognized virtue in schools – and, later, at work!

9. Send your child to school well rested.

10. Send your child to school with a nourishing breakfast under his or her belt. If finances are tight, check with the school to see what in-school assistance programs are available.

11. Make sure your child's clothes have been recently washed and are well pressed.

12. Send your child to school the first day – and every day – equipped to learn. Often this means having things such as a pencil, pen, eraser, and notebook.

13. If possible, be there to meet your child when he or she returns from school. If this is impossible, try to have another responsible adult meet your child. If necessary, see if your child's school has a supervised after-school program. As a last resort, have your latch-key child check in with you by phone when he or she gets home from school.

14. If your child goes to day care or a "sitter" after school, have arrangements made well in advance including notes to the office, teacher, and bus driver. This same advice holds for when your child needs to get off the bus at a spot other than his or her normal location. Confusion as to where a child is to go at the end of the day causes teachers to wonder how much parents really are tuned into their child's life.

15. Attend scheduled parent-teacher's nights. Even if you have to miss reruns of *Seinfeld* or *America's*

Got Talent, it is worth it. If your child is from a two-parent household, it is best if both parents attend. Sign in, shake hands with your child's teacher, review any of your child's work that is on display. Use this brief opportunity to establish positive expectations in the minds of your child's teachers. The teacher will remember which kids' parents showed up and which didn't.

16. Schedule meetings with your child's teachers. These can be used to address a specific concern or to simply get more detailed feedback regarding your child's progress in school.

17. Join and enthusiastically participate in Parent Teacher Associations.

18. Send sincere "thank you notes" or notes of appreciation to your child's teachers when appropriate. Buy a few inexpensive "Thank You" cards. Don't overdo it here.

19. At parent conferences, listen to and work with the classroom teacher, but also take the opportunity to point out some positive, but realistic, traits of your child (e.g., "John has a tremendous memory, he can remember.........") Many times, teachers associate good memory with the ability to learn, hence "planting the seed" that John really can learn.

20. Volunteer to help with field trips. It may mean having to take time off work to do so, but the payoff in influencing the teacher' expectations of your

child can be substantial--and long lasting! Of course, not every parent has such flexibility.

21. Consider your dress when visiting your child's school. I can't stress this point too highly! Stories abound about parents who come to school in cutoff shorts and a dirty tee-shirt, t-shirts with suggestive or violent imprints, low-cut blouses, tight skirts, mini-skirts, etc. Sometimes the need to "come right from work" will necessitate work-related dress. That's fine. Just remember, schools, by and large, are conservative institutions. Until they change (which is not likely to happen soon), parents would be well advised to fit in with school dress norms. Note, most work environments, too, whether they be banking, business, industry, medicine, are conservative.

22. At home, at least when your children are young, "play school," or at least "play" aspects related to what happens in school that can help create positive expectations. Practice a good handshake, good eye contact, taking notes, speaking loud enough to be heard across the room, etc. These are so important that I will repeat them. **Practice a good handshake, good eye contact, taking notes, speaking loud enough to be heard across the room, etc.** Enlist the help of a friend or neighbor. Have your child deliver a note (as is done in school where attendance slips are sent to the office) to a neighbor, or have your child relate a story (as in show-and-tell at school) to a neighbor. These

efforts are confidence building and transfer well to school situations.

23. Encourage your child's pre-school to include, if they don't already, "playing school." Ask them to practice many of the skills that high-expectations students who come to school have already mastered. This will help "level the playing field."

24. Establish a specific time and place for your child to complete his or her homework. Homework should come first; sports, television and other distractions should come second.

25. Help your child with his or her homework, projects, papers, etc. Help, of course, does not mean doing it for him or her. Offer lots and lots of encouragement to bolster his or her efforts. Note I said encouragement I did not say praise. The two words are not synonyms. Praise is usually reserved for a final or completed product or event. Encouragement can be delivered throughout the child's progress towards his or her goal.

26. Stress to your child the importance of submitting work that has been proofread – spelling, grammar, noun/verb agreement. This is so much easier than it ever was with the spell check and grammar checks that are part of computer programs such as Microsoft Word.

27. Be sure to "sign off" on it if so requested by the teacher.

28. Monitor and review your child's homework. Buy a "stamp" of some sort that you can, with an ink pad, stamp the work as having been completed. Make a little bit of a "big deal" about the "stamping."

29. Impress upon your child the importance of following directions when it comes to completing homework, papers, projects, etc. This can go a very long way towards convincing teachers that your child is serious about his or her studies – and later in life, his or her work.

30. Check your child's book bag each evening for notes sent home by the teacher and/or homework assignments that need to be completed. Further, check that nothing questionable is in the book bag that should not be headed to school.

31. Stress the importance of submitting work that is legible – can be read. Keep in mind that teachers have piles of papers every day to score and/or grade. Teachers cannot give a student credit for what they can't read. If at all possible, type or use one of the many word processing programs readily available on computers today. Many schools and libraries have such resources available for limited student use.

32. Encourage your child to ask clarification questions about any assignments that they do not fully understand.

33. Every once in a while, encourage your child to do an "extra" assignment and then submit it to the teacher. The odds are that the teacher will perceive your child as a hard worker and good (maybe even great) student! Once again, don't overdo it.

34. Encourage your child, when possible, to sit closer to the front and center of the classroom. This is the area in which teachers more often direct their teaching, call on students, and recognize raised hands. Research reveals that the these are more favorable seating locations in the minds of instructors.

35. Encourage your child to volunteer, (raise hands first if this is the rule). This can be to answer questions, take attendance slips to the office, or to do any number of things, all of which help to show the teacher that you child is both a willing and able student. And, besides many of these activities are fun!

36. Every parent wants to defend his or her child – I know that my wife and I do. But, at the same time there may be an occasion when a child clearly has misbehaved or otherwise done something wrong in school. This is bound to happen sometime. Help your child to understand that when one is wrong one is wrong and the best thing to do is to admit it, stand tall, and accept the school's reasonable sanction.

37. Buy your child a decent stapler – seriously! It will last a lifetime. Don't use those dinky little red plastic ones where the staple rips out easily. Cheap staplers often leave the pointy ends of the staple sticking out to puncture handlers. It can hurt! Believe me, teachers remember.

38. Instruct your child not to submit papers that are paper-clipped or dog-eared together unless instructed to do so. The paperclips usually fly off into space somewhere or get caught in the mounds of the teacher's other paperwork. The "dog-eared" papers separate too easily.

39. Consider buying a three-hole punch, preferably one that punches slightly larger holes (11/32" rather than 9/32"). The slightly larger holes allow the paper to be turned in your child's ringed notebook without catching / tearing. This three-hole punch will last a lifetime. Further, single-hole punches just do not produce a finished look.

40. Have your child avoid using spiral notebooks (unless instructed to do so) that result in ragged edges when pages are torn out and passed in. These present a "messy" first impression of your child's work. Further, the papers are difficult for the teacher to "register" when tapping the bunch of them on a desk – their frayed edges "catch."

At first, the last several suggestions – good stapler, neat paper edges, papers that turn easily in a ringed notebook, using staples rather than paperclips – may sound a little "Mickey Mouse." But, when a teacher has to score mounds and mounds of homework and other assignments, he or she will take notice of those submissions that present a good first impression! Remember, first impressions are lasting impressions.

Why not have your child's work be of the quality that stands out positively? Further, when a teacher first sees a messy submission, he or she may be likely to think, "Gee, if the student does not even take the time and energy to make the paper / project look good on the surface, how unlikely is it that he or she has paid much attention to what is inside?"

TRY THIS "EXPECTATIONS" TACTIC; IT WORKS REALLY WELL!

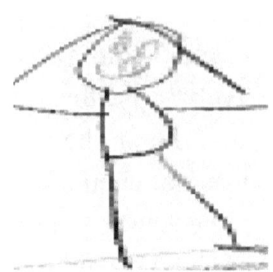

When you ask a child to do something, such as, "Lisa, please wash your hands before we sit down to supper," immediately add the word "Thanks!" Saying the word "Thanks" at the end of your request conveys an expectation that you actually believe that the child is going to comply with your request and, thus, is deserving of your "Thanks" ahead of time. It is harder to ignore a request when the person making the request has already thanked us right up front!

This strategy works even better if, once you have said your "Thanks," you simply turn away or walk away. This makes it extra clear to the child that you have every reason to believe that your reasonable request will be honored and that there is no need for you to stay and monitor the child's compliance. Your "Thanks" and your body language says that you "trust" that the child will comply.

Other examples from home that the reader might recognize include:

- "Joey, would you take out the garbage for me? Thanks!"

- "Wendy, would you help me by setting the table? Thanks, I appreciate it!"

- "David, I need to move several packages from the basement to the garage. Would you give me a hand? I could really use the help!" Thanks!

Still other examples from a school environment might include:

- "Sam, you know the rule about reading comic books in school. Please put them away. Thanks!"

- "Jennifer, would you help me by picking up the art materials and putting them in the boxes on the shelf? That would be a big help. Thanks!"

WHO IS THE PYGMALION? AN EYE-OPENER!

"If you expect the battle to be insurmountable, you've met the enemy. It's you."
(Khang Kijarro Nguyen)

Upon first reading or hearing title, *"Who is the Pygmalion,"* the answer would seem obvious. In a home it would be the parents. In a classroom it would be the teacher. On the sports field it would be the coach. And, in the workplace it would be the boss. Simple. Well, if you agree with the statements above, you would be absolutely right! But you also could be absolutely wrong! How can that be?

The answer lies in the definition of a Pygmalion. A Pygmalion, as used in the Pygmalion Effect, is a phenomenon whereby one person's expectations of a target person affects that the target person's performance. The real eye-opener here is that the Pygmalion Effect works both ways – in a home the parents could be the Pygmalion but just as easily the child could be the Pygmalion. In a school, students could be a Pygmalion imposing their expectations on teachers. Players, too, could be a Pygmalion in the life of their coaches. And, of course, employees could be a Pygmalion for their bosses. This comes as a real shock to some parents, teachers, coaches and bosses who, until realizing it, thought that they, and only they, held the power of expectations!

What it boils down to is that a child's, a student's, a player's and an employee's success can and usually is impacted by the parents', teachers', coaches' and bosses' expectations. It also boils down to the parents', teachers', coaches' and bosses' success can and usually is impacted by the children's, students', players' and employees' expectations. Why is this true? It is true because the power of expectations, the Pygmalion Effect, is a force that exists between human beings no matter their title or station in life. Human beings are human beings – the Pygmalion Effect could care less.

For instance, if a student or group of students felt that a particular teacher was a good teacher, perhaps even a great teacher, they would act towards that teacher in a way that conveyed their high expectations of him or her. They would send all of the signals that this book talks about that convey "I (we) have high expectations of you!" The teacher would pick up on these cues and respond accordingly – e.g., probably even better prepare for the next class, etc.

For some parents, teachers, coaches and bosses it is downright scary to realize that so-called-underlings can have such expectations power over them. Just like a student whose teachers bombarded him or her with negative expectations messages day in and day out would be less likely to succeed, a teacher bombarded with those same kinds of negative messages also would be less likely to succeed. No one is immune from the power of expectations.

CONCLUSION

"Our future expectations must be turned into present
realities."
(James Cone, Theologian)

Expectations formed are, like beauty, "in the eye of
the beholder." This is what makes the situation so
unpredictable. How can a child or a child's parents predict
just what expectations will be formed by teachers?

There is no crystal ball that can be used to
determine ahead of time how your child's teachers will
respond to the many expectation-triggering factors
presented in this book. What we know for sure is that
teachers *WILL* respond to these factors.

The problem may be even more serious because
often more than just one expectation-triggering factor is
operating at any given moment. For instance, a child could
be "of color," "have an unusual name," "be overweight,"
"come from "a bad side of town," **and** "have been preceded
in school by a sibling who was a holy terror." Imagine the
expectations teachers might hold for this child! Or, maybe
you don't want to imagine it.

Help exists for parents in several ways.

- **One**, parents can become more informed about the self-fulfilling process. Information – like that contained in this book – can be converted into power!

- **Two**, parents can stay alert for signs of where their child may be receiving negative expectations-type messages from teachers. Appropriate action then can be taken – including starting right at home!

- **Three**, parents can take preemptive measures by working with schools to help them understand the potential damage that can occur when negative expectations are left unchecked and understand the potential good that can be achieved when positive expectations are conveyed.

LEARNING MORE ABOUT THE POWER OF EXPECTATIONS

Thank you for reading this book, *Giving children the "expectations" advantage*! I hope that it will be useful to you, your family, or to your colleagues. Information regarding the power of expectations should be in the hands of **all** parents, **all** teachers, and **all** child-care workers. In fact, I would like it to be in the hands of brand-new parents – made available to them in the hospital when the child is born.

If you would like to learn more about the self-fulfilling prophecy (e.g., the power of expectations), consider ordering the book, *The Self-Fulfilling prophecy: A Practical Guide to its Use in Education*.

The three most important words in real estate are *location, location, location!* The three most important words in education are *expectations, expectations, expectations!* This 1997, 185-page book is very well referenced and, from reports by readers, very easy to read – complete with cartoons! It contains practitioner testimonials attesting to the need to understand, use, and control the power of expectations in the classroom.

Books by Dr. Robert T. Tauber, PhD

The first set of books are recently published "professional" books – inexpensive, easily read, interesting, a bit fun to read, and immediately useful to parents, teachers, coaches, managers, practitioners, and other professionals!

- *Projecting Enthusiasm: The Key to Dynamic Presentations for Professionals!*

  Being enthusiastic is not enough. One *MUST* project that enthusiasm. But how?

- *Delivering Empathy: Fundamental to Successful Leadership!*

  All successful leaders share one skill – they can deliver empathy to any and all audiences.

- *Praise Less, Encourage More: Judge, Evaluate and Manipulate Less; Fortify, Galvanize, Embolden and Influence More!*

  Praise & encouragement are *NOT* synonyms. Many cautions surround praise. Basically, no cautions exist for encouragement!

- *Negative Reinforcement & Time-Out: Two POSITIVE Classroom Management Strategies*

  Not 1 in 1000 people know the definition of negative reinforcement! Hence, it is overlooked and poorly used.

- *Giving Children the Expectations Advantage: Make the Power of Expectations Work for You!*

  What you expect, you generally get. How can parents and teachers shape these expectations?

- ***Classroom Management: "What A" to "Z" Discipline Strategies: Simple Strategies that WILL Improve Classroom Discipline!***

  These management skills *WILL* improve home & school discipline.

- ***Oral Communication Skills for the Vocational & Technology Workforce: Walk the Walk and Especially Talk the Talk!***

  Vocational & technical workers are *CHEATED* when it comes to this skill.

- ***Using Empathy as Physicians: The What, Why, and How!***

  Patients deserve emphatic doctors. Do you agree?

The next set of books are recently published "personal" books – also inexpensive, easily read, interesting and, at times, contain more than a bit of tongue-and-cheek humor.

- ***From Whence We Came: The Tauber Family History in Photos.***

  Author's family through the ages with pictures.

- ***Yorkshire Pudding, Castles, B&Bs and Pubs: An American Family's 1984-85 Sabbatical in England!***

  Off we went to England for a year with 18 pieces of luggage. We came back with 2 MG-B car fenders!

- ***Inheritance? What Inheritance? We spent it on travel, food, and drink!***

Our children asked why we were saving our money. They said we should spend it. So, we listened to them – we are spending it!

- *Bob's "AUTO" Biography: Are Cars a Reflection of One's Personality?*
  A history of Bob's 40 vehicles from British sports cars to minivans to RVs.

The remaining books are "professional" books that have stood the test of time and continue to be cited in the professional literature – eye-opening, easily read, interesting, and immediately useful.

- *Classroom Management: Sound Theory and Effective Practice* (1st, 2nd, 3rd & 4th ed).
  Note: The 3rd edition was translated into Chinese!

- *Acting Lessons for Teachers: Using Performance Skills in the Classroom.* (1st & 2nd ed).

  Teaching, as well as most professions, must engage, motivate, and inform an audience. But how?

- *Self-Fulfilling Prophecy: A Practical Guide to Its Use in Education.* (and all other fields)
  First impressions are lasting impressions. You get what you expect – good or bad! Control them!

These inexpensive books are available by going to Amazon.com, selecting "books," & then typing in "Robert T. Tauber." Also available as ebooks.
rtt1453@comcast.net

www.ingramcontent.com/pod-product-compliance
Lightning Source LLC
Chambersburg PA
CBHW051347280526
45784CB00007B/2850